AQA  Religious Studies B

Religion and Life Issues

GCSE

Marianne Fleming
Anne Jordan
Peter Smith
David Worden

Series editor
Cynthia Bartlett

 Nelson Thornes

Published in 2009 by:
Nelson Thornes Ltd
Delta Place
27 Bath Road
CHELTENHAM
GL53 7TH
United Kingdom

09 10 11 12 13 / 10 9 8 7 6 5 4 3 2 1

A catalogue record for this book is available from the British Library

ISBN 978 1 4085 0513 7

Cover photograph/illustration by Jess Hurd / reportdigital.co.uk

Illustrations by Hart McLeod and Paul McCaffrey (c/o Sylvie Poggio Agency)

Page make-up by Hart McLeod, Cambridge

Printed and bound in Spain by GraphyCems

Photo acknowledgements
Alamy: Adrian Sherratt / 1.2D; ArkReligion.com / 1.8D; Camera Lucida Environment / 2.5B; Chuck Nacke /
4.8B; David Hoffman Photo Library / 3.1B; Jason Baxter / 5.8A; Jeffrey Blacker / 1.7E; Parleycoot Celebrity
and Personality Images / 3.10C; Trinty Mirror / Mirrorpix / 1.10A; World Religions Photo Library / 4.8C; **Boys
Brigade**: 6.4B; **CAFOD**: Paul Jeffrey / 2.10B; 2.10D; **Corbis**: Bettmann / 3.8A; **Fotolia**: 1.1E; 1.5A; 1.5B; 1.5C;
1.5G; 1.6A; 1.6B; 1.7C; 1.7D; 1.8A1; 1.8A2 2.1A; 2.1B; 2.2A; 2.2B; 2.3B; 2.5C; 2.6B; 2.7B; 2.7D; 2.8A; 2.9C;
2.9D; 2.9E; 2.10A; 3.1A; 3.3B; 3.3C; 3.3D; 3.3F; 3.4A; 3.4B; 3.4E; 3.4F; 3.4G; 3.5B; 3.6A; 3.8C; 3.8D; 4.1B;
4.1C; 4.2A; 4.2D; 4.3B; 4.3C; 4.3D 4.4A; 4.4B; 4.5A; 4.5B; 4.7A; 4.7C; 4.10A; 5.1A; 5.1C; 5.2A; 5.2B; 5.3A;
5.3B; 5.4C; 5.5A; 5.5B; 5.6A; 5.8D; 5.9B; 6.1A; 6.2B; 6.2C; 6.3B; 6.3C; 6.4A; 6.5A; 6.5B; 6.6A; 6.7B; 6.7C;
6.8A; 6.9C; 6.11A; **Getty Images**: 1.2C; 3.1C; 3.7C; 3.9A; 3.9B; 4.6A; 4.6B; 5.9C; AFP / 3.7B; Popperfoto /
3.10B; 5.1B1; 5.1B2; Time & Life Pictures / 5.10A; WireImage / 3.3G; **Girls Brigade**: 6.4C; **iStockphoto**: 1.1A;
1.1B; 1.1C; 1.1D; 1.1F; 1.1G; 1.2A; 1.2B; 1.3A; 1.3B; 1.3C; 1.4A; 1.4B; 1.4C; 1.4D; 1.5D; 1.5E; 1.5F; 1.7A;
1.7B; 1.8C; 1.9A; 1.9B; 1.9D; 1.10B; 2.3A; 2.4A; 2.4B; 2.4C; 2.5A; 2.6A; 2.6C; 2.6E; 2.7E; 2.8B; 2.8C; 2.9A;
2.9B; 3.2A; 3.2C; 3.2D; 3.3A; 3.3E; 3.4C; 3.4D; 3.6B; 3.6C; 3.7A; 4.1A; 4.1D; 4.2B; 4.2C; 4.3A; 4.5C; 4.7B;
4.9A; 4.9D; 4.11A; 5.1D; 5.2C; 5.4A; 5.4B; 5.6B; 5.7A; 5.8B; 5.9A; 5.10B; 5.10C; 5.11A; 6.2A; 6.3A; 6.6B;
6.6C; 6.6D; 6.7A; 6.7D; 6.8B; 6.9A; 6.9B; 6.10A; 6.10B; **PaxChristi**: 5.3C; **PeaceMaker**: 5.2D; **Photolibrary**:
The British Library / 2.1C; The Print Collector / 4.8A **Rex Features**: 3.2B; 3.5A; 3.5C; East News / 5.8C; **Still
Pictures**: Adrian Arbib / 2.10C.

Text acknowledgements
Scripture quotations taken from the Holy Bible, New International Version. Copyright © 1978, 1984 by
International Bible Society. Used by permission of Hodder & Stoughton, a division of Hodder Headline Ltd. All
rights reserved. "NIV" is a registered trademark of International Bible Society. UK trademark number 1448790.

1.9: Headline, 'Warlords turn to ivory trade to fund slaughter of humans', Independent, Monday March 17
2008. Reprinted with permission.
2.4: Short extract adapted from 'Traffic hell' predicted with 6m more cares by 2031' by Dan Milmo, The
Guardian, Monday September 10 2007. Copyright © Guardian News & Media Ltd 2007. Used with permission.
2.9: Crown Copyright materials reproduced with permission of the controller of the HMSO.
3.10: Short extract from HOPE AND SUFFERING by Desmond Tutu, Eerdmans, 1985. Reprinted with
permission.
4.5: Short quote by Armin A. Brott. © Armin A. Brott. Reprinted with kind permission of the author.
4.7 & 5.4: Extracts from THE HOLY QURAN TRANSLATION AND COMMENTARY by Abdullah Yusuf Ali.
Reprinted with permission of IPCI - Islamic Vision, 434 Coventry Road, Small Heath, Birmingham B10 0UG UK.
5.2: Short extract from LOOKING INWARDS, LOOKING OUTWARDS ed, Joyce Mackley (CEM 1997). Reprinted
with permission.
6.10: Crown copyright material is reproduced with the permission of the Controller of HMSO.

Contents

Nelson Thornes has worked in partnership with AQA to make sure that this book offers you the best possible support for your GCSE course. All the content has been approved by the senior examining team at AQA, so you can be sure that it gives you just what you need when you are preparing for your exams.

How to use this book

This book covers everything you need for your course.

Learning Objectives

At the beginning of each section or topic you'll find a list of Learning Objectives based on the requirements of the specification, so you can make sure you are covering everything you need to know for the exam.

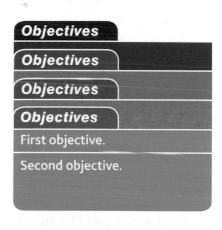

AQA Examiner's Tips

Don't forget to look at the AQA Examiner's Tips throughout the book to help you with your study and prepare for your exam.

> **AQA Examiner's tip**
>
> Don't forget to look at the AQA Examiner's Tips throughout the book to help you with your study and prepare for your exam.

AQA Examination-style Questions

These offer opportunities to practise doing questions in the style that you can expect in your exam so that you can be fully prepared on the day.

AQA examination questions are reproduced by permission of the Assessment and Qualifications Alliance.

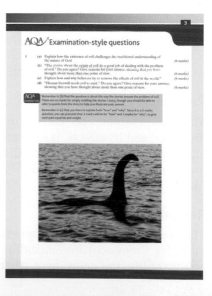

AQA ↗ GCSE Religion and Life Issues

This book is written specifically for GCSE students studying the AQA Religious Studies Specification B, *Unit 2 Religion and Life Issues*. The course encourages thinking about the connections between religion and issues people face in life, including animal life and environmental issues, prejudice, the right to life, war and peace, and religion and young people.

The course will help you develop your knowledge and understanding of religion by exploring the impact of religious beliefs and values on moral behaviour. You will explore the views of believers in one or more of the six major world religions and develop your skills in evaluating them and in explaining your own reasoned opinions.

■ Topics in this unit

In the examination you must answer four questions, based on four of the following six topics.

Religion and animal rights

This topic examines religious ideas about human responsibility for other species and the contemporary use and abuse of animals including the treatment of wildlife, and uses of animals for companions, food, sport, profit and experimentation.

Religion and planet Earth

This topic explores religious beliefs about the origins of life and human responsibility for its preservation. It investigates environmental problems and the work being done to look after the world.

Religion and prejudice

This topic examines the causes, origins and forms of prejudice and its effects. It explores religious beliefs and responses to prejudice and discrimination, including the work of religious believers who have fought against prejudice.

Religion and early life

This topic explores religious beliefs that influence attitudes about abortion, including the sanctity and quality of life, the question of when life begins, the legal rights of those involved and alternatives to abortion.

Religion, war and peace

This topic examines religious beliefs that influence attitudes to war, the causes and effects of war, the criteria for 'Just' and 'holy wars', pacifism and religious responses to war and peace.

Religion and young people

This topic explores faith among the young, including initiation and coming of age ceremonies; moral codes; faith groups, activities and festivals; the roles of school and home; and the problems and benefits of a religious upbringing.

■ Assessment guidance

The questions set in the examination will allow you to refer in your answers to the religion(s) you have studied. To encourage you to practise examination-type questions, each chapter has an assessment guidance section at the end. Each question in the examination will include a three-mark and a six-mark evaluation question. It will help you to write better answers yourself, if you understand what the examiners are looking for when they mark these questions. To assist you in this, you will be asked to mark a sample answer of a six-mark question for yourself – using the mark scheme opposite. Make sure that you understand the differences between the standard of answer for each level, and what you need to do to achieve full marks.

Examination questions will test two assessment objectives

AO1	Describe, explain and analyse, using knowledge and understanding.	50%
AO2	Use evidence and reasoned argument to express and evaluate personal responses, informed insights, and differing viewpoints.	50%

The examiner will also take into account the quality of your written communication – how clearly you express yourself and how well you communicate your meaning. The grid on page 7 also gives you some guidance on the sort of quality examiners expect to see at different levels.

Levels of response mark scheme for six-mark evaluation questions

Levels	Criteria for AO1	Criteria for AO2	Quality of written communication	Marks
0	Nothing relevant or worthy of credit	An unsupported opinion or no relevant evaluation	The candidate's presentation, spelling punctuation and grammar seriously obstruct understanding	0 marks
Level 1	Something relevant or worthy of credit	An opinion supported by simple reason	The candidate presents some relevant information in a simple form. The text produced is usually legible. Spelling, punctuation and grammar allow meaning to be derived, although errors are sometimes obstructive	1 mark
Level 2	Elementary knowledge and understanding, e.g. two simple points	An opinion supported by one developed or two simple reasons		2 marks
Level 3	Sound knowledge and understanding	An opinion supported by one well developed reason or several simple reasons. **N.B. Candidates who make no religious comment should not achieve more than Level 3**	The candidate presents relevant information in a way which assists with the communication of meaning. the text produced is legible. Spelling, punctuation and grammar are sufficiently accurate not to obscure meaning	3 marks
Level 4	A clear knowledge and understanding with some development	An opinion supported by two developed reasons with reference to religion		4 marks
Level 5	A detailed answer with some analysis, as appropriate	Evidence of reasoned consideration of two different points of view, showing informed insights and knowledge and understanding of religion	The candidate presents relevant information coherently, employing structure and style to render meaning clear. The text produced is legible. Spelling, punctuation and grammar are sufficiently accurate to render meaning clear	5 marks
Level 6	A full and coherent answer showing good analysis, as appropriate	A well-argued response, with evidence of reasoned consideration of two different points of view showing informed insights and ability to apply knowledge and understanding of religion effectively		6 marks

Note: In evaluation answers to questions worth only 3 marks, the first three levels apply. Questions which are marked out of 3 marks do not ask for two views, but reasons for your own opinion.

Successful study of this unit will result in a Short Course GCSE award. Study of one further unit will provide a Full Course GCSE award. Other units in Specification B which may be taken to achieve a Full Course GCSE award are:

- Unit 1 Religion and Citizenship
- Unit 3 Religion and Morality
- Unit 4 Religious Philosophy and Ultimate Questions
- Unit 5 Religious Expression in Society
- Unit 6 Worship and Key Beliefs

1.1 Animals and humans

How are animals different from humans?

Activities

1. Before working through this section, with a partner, in a small group or as a class, make a list of ways in which humans are 'better' than animals.

2. In your opinion, what are animals for?

In one sense humans **are** animals. The theory of evolution describes life developing over millions of years, from tiny single-celled creatures into more and more complex varieties of animals, and finally humans. Humans share many biological features with animals – a reason for the use of animals in research.

Most people believe that humans are on a higher level than animals. Religions have tended to support this idea. With the possible exception of Buddhism, all religions have taught that God created animals for a purpose, to be of value and support to humans. Those who believe in reincarnation think being reborn as an animal is punishment for past misdeeds. In both cases, animals are on a lower level to humans.

Human intelligence – animal instinct

Human intelligence, the ability to make decisions, form opinions and think about the consequences of actions, sets us apart from animals. Animals seem to behave according to their instincts to survive, eat and reproduce. They do not seem to have the ability to reason. Humans can read and write, understand ideas and communicate their opinions to others. They can give reasons for what they think. An animal cannot do that. Even though many animals communicate with others (whales and birds, for example), they do not give reasons for what they think.

Although some animals live in complex societies (bees and ants, for example), they do this to survive rather than to create a good quality of life. Although scientists have found some instances of seemingly selfless animal behaviour (such as protecting their young so the species survives), many will abandon the weakest member of the herd. Most humans protect the weak and vulnerable. Humans can act in a moral way, choosing to be good or bad. They create art, music and literature, and develop and use science and technology.

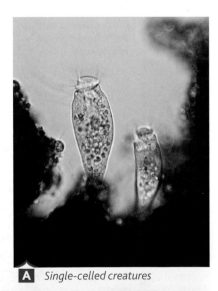

A Single-celled creatures

B Bees create a complex hive to survive, but humans can create complex technology to improve their quality of life

Animals do not have religious beliefs. They do not worship or communicate with God, or follow the kind of moral code of behaviour that allows people to live happily together in society. Believers are not all agreed about whether animals have souls and it is impossible to know. Those who believe in reincarnation think an animal's body holds a soul that will inhabit another body when the animal dies. Most people who believe in some sort of life after death think the afterlife only applies to humans.

How should we treat animals?

Most people would say that just because the status of animals is lower than that of humans, does not mean humans should mistreat them. Most would agree that humans can use animals to help us to live without harming the life of the animals. Religions teach that although animals are not equal to humans, they should be cared for and respected as part of the natural world.

Activities

3 Explain three ideas about the way religions see the place of animals in the world. Does this affect your previous answer in question 2?

4 With a partner, or in a small group, list 10 ways in which humans use animals. Which ways are acceptable and which are not? Explain your opinions, and refer to religious thinking. Try to think about how you decided which uses are acceptable and which are not. The images may help you.

C *Some ways in which humans use animals*

links

More detail on religious teachings on animals is given throughout this chapter.

AQA Examiner's tip

Remember, religions do **not** say animals are equal to humans. The specification talks about the 'status' of animals and their 'relative value'. This means whether or not they are of less importance than humans and should be treated differently as a result.

Summary

You should now be able to explain how animals are different from humans, some religious ideas about their place in the world (their relative status and value) and whether this makes a difference to the way humans treat animals.

Do animals have rights?

Rights

The term 'animal rights' was first used in 1892. There are now hundreds of organisations to protect the rights of animals. These organisations believe that animals deserve to live according to their own nature and not be harmed, exploited or abused. Animal rights' campaigners say animals have a dignity and have the same rights as humans to be free from cruelty and exploitation. Many oppose factory farming, animal experimentation and using animals for entertainment. Not all animal rights' supporters agree about whether research on animals should ever take place. There is also disagreement about what kinds of protests are justified in order to stand up for animal rights.

Objectives

Explore the concept of 'animal rights'.

Understand some religious views on how the rights of animals should be protected.

 Should animals be factory farmed or used in experiments?

 links

For more about factory farming see page 18 and the Glossary. For more about animal experimentation, see page 26 and the Glossary.

Discussion activity

1   Should laws protect animals just like humans? Discuss in pairs or small groups, trying to see different points of view.

Protecting the rights of animals

Animal rights' groups have had some success in changing public attitudes and the law. Some groups celebrate International Animal Rights Day each year on December 10th, the day on which the UN published its Declaration of Human Rights in 1948. Campaigners think animals should have similar rights of protection from exploitation and suffering as humans. Candlelit vigils, protest marches and letters to MPs are all used to highlight the issues. However, some groups have taken more direct and even violent action, breaking into laboratories and releasing animals held there for research or targeting individuals who work in animal research facilities.

Animal welfare groups like the World Wide Fund for Nature (WWF) or the Royal Society for the Prevention of Cruelty to Animals (RSPCA) raise awareness and monitor the treatment of animals.

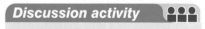 links

For more about the WWF and the RSPCA see page 15.

Discussion activity

2   With a partner or in a small group, discuss the following statement, giving reasons for your opinion.

'People have the right to do what they want to animals.'

Protecting animals by law

British law protects animals from cruelty and neglect, which are criminal offences. Some living creatures cannot be kept as pets, for example dangerous dogs or rare birds. Animal experiments to research cosmetics are banned. Legal experiments for medical and other research are inspected to make sure animals are not suffering too much. Foxhunting and dog fighting are illegal and there are strict regulations about animal exports, transporting animals for slaughter and the management of abattoirs (where animals are slaughtered).

Religious attitudes

Religions do not teach that animals have the same rights as humans, but that they should be protected, managed and cared for with respect. All religions except Buddhism, believe God created the world and therefore it deserves respect. Humans do not own the planet, but have a sacred duty to care for it (stewardship). The idea of the **sanctity of life** (including animals) influences their views. Humans have **responsibility** for the way they use their power over the natural world.

Most religious believers would support the kind of work animal welfare groups do. However, religious people may be divided about the means people use to defend animal rights. Most would accept non-violent lawful protest. Some would say actions such as trespassing or causing damage to property may be justified in extreme cases. Most would not accept violent protest that caused harm to human beings.

Animal rights' protesters

Two farmers in Staffordshire who were breeding guinea pigs for medical research suffered five years of abuse and intimidation. Their families received death threats, letter bombs and their property was constantly being damaged. The grave of one man's mother-in-law was dug up and her remains stolen. Although an animal rights' group condemned this action, they still protested regularly outside the farm. The local area was covered with abusive graffiti, local pubs were attacked and explosives were let off at night, leaving local residents sleepless. The police recorded over 450 separate incidents. The farmers stopped breeding guinea pigs. Four protestors were eventually jailed.

Case study

B *Religious people may support animal rights but may not agree about the means of defending them*

Key terms

Sanctity of life: life is sacred because it is God-given.

Responsibility: duty; the idea that we are in charge of our own actions.

⚭ **links**

See page 34 and the Glossary for more on stewardship.

Research activity 🔍

Using the internet or a library, find out how other animal rights' campaigners protest on behalf of animals. Record your findings to use as examples in the examination. You could create a table listing the groups, what their aims are, and the methods they use.

Discussion activity 👥

3 Using the pictures on this page, the case study and the information you found in the research activity, discuss the following questions in small groups; to explain your opinions.

a How far should religious people go in defending animal rights?

b Are some of the methods used by animal rights' campaigners wrong? Explain your opinion.

AQA *Examiner's tip*

Remember, religious people support animal welfare and rights, but they differ about **how** the rights of animals are protected.

Summary

You should now be able to explain some religious views on animal rights and the means of protecting those rights.

■ Religious views

Objectives

Explore religious beliefs and teachings about animals.

Buddhism

Buddhists attach great importance to the natural world. They see all living beings as connected to and dependent on each other for survival. Animals should be treated well because they are part of the cycle of rebirth. Buddhism is a religion of love and compassion and the first moral precept, not to harm any living thing, applies to animals. Buddhists practice meditation to develop feelings of loving kindness towards all living beings, all of whom have the same right to happiness.

Hinduism

Hindus believe in the sanctity of all life. All creatures should be respected because they are part of Brahman (God). All living things are bound up in the cycle of birth, death and rebirth as the soul is reborn in different forms. Hindus have a duty to protect animals and not to harm them. Many Hindu deities have animals as their vehicles or appear in animal form. The cow is sacred in Hinduism and is allowed to roam free in India.

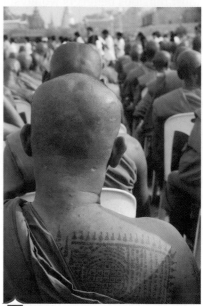

A   Buddhists believe animals should be treated well because they are part of the the cycle of rebirth

B   The cow is sacred in Hinduism

Christianity

Christians believe God created the world, including animals and people, and put humans in charge (Genesis 1:28). Christians believe they have a duty to care for all creation, including animals. Jesus spoke about the value of every living creature, even each individual sparrow (Luke 12:6).

C   Jesus spoke of the value of all creatures even each sparrow

Islam

Muslims believe the world belongs to its Creator Allah who appointed humans as stewards or trustees over it. This means they must care for animals and treat them with respect. Animals have feelings and purpose in their lives and those who are cruel to them will answer to Allah. Muslims have rules about food. They cannot eat pigs and all other animals must be killed in a painless way (halal slaughter). Guidelines about how to treat animals are given in shari'ah law.

Judaism

God created the Earth and gave humans responsibility for its care. Although God gives people 'dominion' over all living creatures, animals should be treated fairly. In the story of Noah, all animal species were saved from the flood, showing the worth of all animals. After the flood, God tells Noah that animals may be his food (Genesis 9:2–3), but prohibits cruelty to them. Jews have food rules that specify which foods they are allowed to eat and how to kill animals by shechitah (ritual slaughter).

Sikhism

God created the Earth and dwells in all things, including animal life. Humans are the custodians of the natural world. It is part of a Sikh's duty to look after animals and not abuse them. Humans will be judged on their treatment of animals.

D *Animals must be killed painlessly (Halal slaughtered)*

Beliefs and teachings

The fear and dread of you will fall upon all the beasts of the earth and all the birds of the air, upon every creature that moves along the ground and upon all the fish of the sea; they are given into your hands. Everything that lives and moves will be food for you. Just as I gave you the green plants, I now give you everything.

Genesis 9:2–3

Activity

1 Without using any reference material, answer the following questions. When you have finished, check your answers using the information on these pages.

a In what ways are all living beings dependent on each other, as Buddhists believe?

b Explain how a religious believer might use the ideas of stewardship (the sacred duty of humans to take care of the world) in arguments about animals' rights.

c Explain how a religious believer might use the idea of sanctity of life in arguments about animals' rights.

links

See page 34 and the Glossary for more on stewardship, the duty of care for the world given to humans

Research activities

1 Using the internet, find out more about the religious food laws mentioned above. (You could also read page 21 related to food laws.)

2 How easy do you think it is for people to follow religious food laws nowadays? Explain your opinion, making notes on key points that you can use in your preparation for the examination.

Summary

You should now be able to explain the religious beliefs and teachings about animals of at least one religion.

AQA Examiner's tip

You need to know the beliefs and teachings of at least one religion that influences believers' attitudes on the different issues raised in this chapter. Use this information in the examination to support your answers.

Zoos, safari parks and aquariums

In support

Many people can remember a trip to a zoo, safari park or aquarium with delight. Visitors can see wild animals close up that they would otherwise never see except on television or in films. Sharks, stingrays and even killer whales are dangerous but fascinating creatures that can be safely seen in an aquarium. Poisonous snakes, butterflies, rare birds and magnificent animals like lions, tigers, elephants and giraffes could not be seen by most people in Britain outside a zoo or safari park. Most zoos have educational activities or areas where children can see some animals up close. Breeding programmes in zoos have helped to save rare species from **extinction**. Some zoos pay for research into animals. This helps us to understand their place in the ecosystem and aid their protection in the wild.

A

In opposition

On the other hand, some zoos and safari parks do not always provide a suitable environment for wild animals. Sometimes animals are kept in small cages and suffer stress. The climate and habitat is often different from their native environment and some animals find it difficult to adjust. Several years ago a polar bear in a New York zoo was reported to be showing distress because of the very hot summer temperatures.

Religious views

Most religious people accept zoos if the animals are kept in conditions that are as near as possible to life in the wild. Many zoos and safari parks closely recreate the natural habitat of species and allow animals to roam over large areas. Religious people recognise that zoos can help preserve species in the wild by research and through carefully designed breeding programmes.

B

C

Religious responses

Assisi Declarations

On the 25th anniversary of the creation of the WWF (1986), leaders of all six major world religions met in Assisi, Italy, the home of St Francis, the patron saint of animals. Leaders from each religion made statements about how people should act responsibly for the welfare of the Earth, including animals.

Ohito Declaration

In 1995, at a similar conference in Ohito, Japan, world religious leaders issued some spiritual principles:

- Religions recognise the need to treat the environment, including animals, with care.
- Sustaining environmental life is a religious responsibility.
- Nature needs to be treated with respect and compassion.

Practical action

The RSPCA was started in 1824 by the Reverend Arthur Broome and other Christians in response to cruelty to animals. It was the world's first animal welfare organisation. Today there are a great many conservation and animal welfare organisations, such as Greenpeace and WWF, that are supported by religious believers. There are also religious environmental organisations, such as the Islamic Foundation for Ecology and Environmental Sciences, Quaker Concern for Animals, and the Anglican Society for the Welfare of Animals.

Endangered species

Case study

The hawksbill turtle has lost over 80 per cent of its global population. The turtles are taken to make tortoiseshell items like frames for sunglasses and jewellery. There are about 8,000 turtles left. Some drown when they are caught in fishing nets. The building of tourist hotels and marinas next to beaches has made it difficult for females to nest and lay their eggs. Pollution has also caused deaths. Turtles swallow or get tangled in plastic bags. Stranded turtles have been found to have poisonous metals in them or in their eggs.

D *There are only about 8,000 hawksbill turtles left*

links

Find out more at:

www.rspca.org.uk
www.greenpeace.org.uk
www.wwf.org.uk
www.ifees.org.uk
www.quaker-animals.org.uk
www.aswa.org.uk

Research activities

1. Choose one or more of the websites listed above and find out more about the organisations work and their beliefs.

2. Record and share your findings with your group. Explain whether their work supports the religious principles outlined at Ohito.

Activity

3. 'Religious people should be more concerned about helping humans than about preserving endangered species.' Do you agree? Give reasons for your answer, showing that you have thought about more than one point of view.

AQA Examiner's tip

In answering questions on religious responses to the preservation of species from extinction, refer to the material here and also to the section on the fur and ivory trades.

links

For the fur and ivory trade, see pages 24–25 and the Glossary.

Summary

You should now be able to explain arguments for and against zoos and discuss religious responses to the preservation of species from extinction.

1.5 Useful animals

Pets

Most people who keep pets grow to love them and treat them as a member of the family. For people who live on their own, a pet can provide companionship and a way of expressing affection. Dogs bring many benefits to their owners, including exercise and social contact with other dog walkers. Some people go so far as to dress their pets in designer outfits or have a pet buried in a special cemetery when they die.

A *Pet lovers may buy designer outfits or bury their pet in a special cemetery*

Guide dogs are trained from puppies to help blind and partially sighted people lead more independent lives by helping them cross roads and get around outside their homes. A guide dog's working life is around seven years. After that they retire to a good home. They are both pets and working animals.

Religious views of pets

Most religions do not forbid people to have pets, but in Islam animals must not be kept in limited spaces or trained to perform tricks. Most Muslims, therefore, do not have pets, but can keep working dogs for hunting or guarding their home. In all faiths humane treatment of animals is expected.

Transport and work

Animals are used all over the world to transport people and goods. 'Beasts of burden' like donkeys, mules, camels or horses can be ridden or harnessed to pull carts to carry goods. Dogs are used in the Arctic to pull sleds. Before modern transport was invented, the horse and carriage was a common sight in Britain.

Horses and working dogs are used on farms and oxen or buffalo may be used to pull a plough. In India elephants are used for logging, and in China birds called cormorants are used to catch fish. Guide dogs are not the only animals to help disabled people; small African monkeys have been trained to do simple household tasks like opening mail. 'Sniffer' dogs are used by the police to follow a trail and seek out drugs, and animals are used by the military to locate mines. Dogs carried messages across the trenches during World War I and some were given medals for bravery.

Objectives

Explore the use of animals for companionship, transport and work.

Understand religious attitudes to the use of animals in these ways.

Activity

1 Survey your class to find out the following information.

a Which students have pets and what kind of pets do they have?

b What benefits do they get from keeping an animal as a pet?

c Does it differ with the type of animal, for example a goldfish as opposed to a dog?

AQA Examiner's tip

You need to consider whether using animals for companionship, transport or work is a good or bad use of animals. You must be prepared to explain both sides of this issue and include a religious perspective.

B   *Animals at work*

Religious views of working animals

Most religions do not object to using animals for work or transport as long as they are cared for. Islam teaches that working animals must not beaten or overworked. They must be well-fed and watered. Hindus regard the cow as sacred. The cow gives life by providing food, fuel for heating and a means of transport. More recently, people have realised that contact with animals can bring a therapeutic (helpful to healing) effect to children with autism, sick people, the elderly and prisoners. Most religious people would support the use of animals to heal in this way.

C   *Animals can be therapeutic for cancer patients*

Discussion activity

Split into three groups. Each group should discuss one of the following issues, drawing on both religious teachings and their own views. After the discussions, the groups should report back to the class as a whole on their opinions.

- 'Is there a moral difference between keeping a dog (a tame animal) and keeping a monkey (a wild animal) to help a disabled person?'
- 'It is wrong to use animals for transport or work.'
- 'Treating a pet as if it is human is disrespectful to animals.'

Research activity

Using the internet or a library, find out how dogs are trained to help blind and partially sighted people.

Is this use of an animal justified from a religious point of view? Explain the reasons for your opinion.

D   *Guide dogs are both pets and working animals*

Summary

You should now be able to explain how animals are used by humans for companionship, transport and work and discuss whether these uses of animals are right or wrong, including a religious perspective on the issues.

links

Find out more at:
www.guidedogs.org.uk

Animals for food

Eating meat

Ask someone what a typical British meal is and they might answer fish and chips or a Sunday roast. Many people have been brought up eating meat. They enjoy the taste and for them it is their main source of protein. Livestock farming and fishing are important British industries, so beef, ham, pork, bacon, lamb, poultry and fish are produced and eaten in large quantities.

What are the issues?

Some people object to killing animals for meat and say humans have no right to deprive another living being of life.

Others accept that domesticated animals bred specifically for meat production can be used for food. They are obviously not endangered species, so as long as they are treated well during their lives and killed humanely. These people believe this is morally acceptable.

However, as agriculture has grown into a huge industry, the methods used to produce meat have changed. This has made some people question whether the animals are being mistreated and suffer unnecessary pain or distress in the process.

Free-range versus factory farming

Objectives

Explore the different ways in which meat is produced and transported.

Understand religious attitudes to issues arising from this treatment of animals.

⚭ links

See pages 20–21 for more on the issue of killing animals for meat.

A *Free-range hens*

B *Factory-farmed hens*

Free-range farming

Free-range farming is a method of raising animals so that they can roam freely and live a more natural life. Hens can scratch in the farmyard and are only kept inside at night. Other animals are outdoors and can graze. A free-range dairy cow will stay with her calf, developing a strong bond, while it feeds for six to eight months. Free-range products, however, are usually more expensive to buy.

Key terms

Free-range farming: farming that allows the animals to roam free and behave naturally.

Factory farming

Factory farming is a method of raising animals intensively. A high output of animals can be produced and more profit can be made. Factory farms need to use antibiotics and pesticides to prevent disease because of the crowded living conditions. Animals are kept indoors, sometimes in the dark. Their movement is restricted and they cannot follow their natural behaviour to mate or graze. They may be given growth hormones to make them grow faster or yield more milk or eggs. A factory-farmed cow is separated from her calf shortly after birth and given special food that makes her produce ten times as much milk as she would need for her calf.

The advantages of factory farming are that food production is more efficient and costs less, so meat, milk or eggs can be sold at lower prices to the consumer. Opponents say factory farming threatens animal welfare, human health and the environment. The crowded living conditions cause suffering and distress. The drugs and chemicals used may build up in the food chain and affect human health and resistance to disease. Waste from such farms can get into human water supplies and rivers, killing fish and other wildlife.

Slaughter and transport of animals

In Britain, animals are usually stunned first and then slaughtered (killed). The aim is to let the animal bleed out before death so the meat will be good. Muslim and Jewish methods (halal and shechitah) involve cutting the animal's neck with a sharp knife.

Some animals are sent to be slaughtered many miles away from where they were produced. Animals are transported over long distances in cramped, overcrowded conditions without enough food or water. Many die in transit. Animal welfare groups like the RSPCA campaign for animals to be slaughtered as close as possible to where they were raised.

> **Key terms**
>
> **Factory farming**: when animals are used for meat or dairy products, but are kept indoors in very small spaces.

> **Discussion activity**
>
> 1   With a partner or in a small group, discuss the following statement. Try to consider the moral issues as well as the cost.
>
> 'Free-range farming will make food too expensive.'

> **links**
>
> Find out more about the RSPCA on page 15.

> **Discussion activity**
>
> 2   Using the information on these pages, and what you have learnt about religious attitudes to animals in the previous sections, discuss these issues. Explain your reasons for your opinions.
>
> a   Are the ways that animals are reared, transported and slaughtered humane?
>
> b   Would fewer people eat meat if they thought about how an animal is produced and killed?

> **AQA Examiner's tip**
>
> You need to know the difference between factory and free-range farming and why there is moral debate over which methods should be used.

> **Activities**
>
> 1   Explain the difference between factory farming and free-range farming.
>
> 2   In Britain, some people eat lamb, but would not consider eating dog meat. Should some animals never be used for food?
>
> 3   Based on your knowledge of one religion's teachings, explain what attitudes you think religious believers might take to factory and free-range farming, and the slaughter and transport of animals.

> **Summary**
>
> You should now be able to explain the difference between factory and free-range farming and discuss the issues raised for religious believers by these methods of farming and the slaughter and transport of animals.

Should people eat meat?

Some facts about meat

Ninety per cent of people in the UK are meat eaters. Meat is a good source of protein, vitamins and minerals, particularly vitamin B12 which is only found in foods from animals, such as meat and milk.

Vegetarian and vegan diets

Vegetarianism means a person does not eat fish, animals or birds. A **vegan** refuses to use **any** animal products, including dairy products (milk, cheese, eggs) or fur and leather that comes from a dead animal.

A *Which way of eating appeals to you the most?*

Some reasons why people choose to be vegetarian or vegan include:

- They do not wish to harm animals.
- It is part of their religion.
- They may object to the way meat and poultry are produced and transported.
- They think vegetables, particularly those grown organically, are safer and healthier to eat.
- They do not like the taste of meat.

Many vegetarians argue that if fewer people ate meat, there would be enough food to stop hunger in developing countries. If the large areas of land used to produce a relatively small amount of beef were used instead to grow crops for food, 10 times as many people could be fed.

Objectives

Explore the reasons why some people eat meat and others are vegetarians or vegans.

Understand religious attitudes about eating meat.

Key terms

Vegetarianism: the belief held by people who do not eat meat.

Vegan: a person who will not use any animal product.

∞ links

Read more about meat production and transport on pages 18–19.

B *Beef cattle need much more land than crops. 100 million more people could be fed if meat-eating was reduced by 10 per cent*

Religious attitudes

Most Buddhists and Hindus are vegetarian. They regard animals as part of the cycle of birth, death and rebirth. To them, killing an animal might mean killing a body that houses an ancestor's soul. They believe in the principle of ahimsa, or not harming living creatures.

Buddhist monks will not refuse meat if offered but would not kill an animal themselves. Buddhist scriptures say that living creatures should not be killed, treated with violence, nor abused or tormented (Anchoranga Sutra).

The Vedas (Hindu holy books) say that Hindus should avoid meat because it cannot be obtained without harming living creatures. Some Hindus do eat meat but never any part of a cow, which is a sacred animal.

Many Sikhs are vegetarian and the langar in the gurdwara serves only vegetarian food so as not to offend anyone who may use it. Sikhs may eat meat provided the animals are treated and killed humanely. The Guru Granth Sahib teaches that all food is pure because God provided it for people.

Although individual Christians, Muslims and Jews may be vegetarians for reasons given above, the religions themselves do not teach people to avoid meat. All three religions believe animals were created by God to provide humans with food. After the great flood God told Noah that people may eat animals. St Paul wrote to the Romans that all foods could be eaten, but that Christians should not eat anything that causes someone else to sin.

Muslims and Jews have food laws that tell them which animals they may eat and how to kill them. Muslims eat only halal meat, killed in a humane way 'in the name of Allah, the merciful, the compassionate'. Neither Muslims nor Jews eat pigs. The Qur'an teaches that carrion, blood and pork are forbidden. Jews follow kosher (dietary) laws and do not mix dairy and meat foods. The Torah allows Jews to eat any animal that has a split hoof completely divided and that chews the cud, and fish with fins and scales.

Activity

1 Answer the following questions, and then check your answers against the information in this section.

a Explain the difference between a vegetarian and a vegan diet.

b Explain some of the reasons why some people become vegetarians. Refer to the teaching of one religion in your answer.

Discussion activity

Discuss the statement below in pairs. What do you think? Explain your opinions and make notes on key points that you can use in revision.

'It is not cruel to kill an animal for meat.'

AQA Examiner's tip

You need to know religious reasons as well as other reasons why some people do not eat meat. Be sure you can explain at least one religion's rules about diet or attitude towards eating meat.

Summary

You should now be able to explain why some people eat meat and others are vegetarians or vegans and the religious beliefs that influence attitudes towards these issues.

C A kosher 'deli' prepares food according to Jewish dietary laws.

1.8 Animals in sport

Using animals in sport

Throughout history people have used animals in sport to:

- compete with the animals against opponents (as in horseracing, polo or show jumping)
- watch animals compete against each other (as in greyhound or pigeon racing)
- compete against animals (such as in rodeos and bullfighting).

Arguments for and against using animals in sport

> ANIMALS FEEL PAIN AND FEAR. IT'S WRONG TO USE THEM FOR OUR ENTERTAINMENT.

> ANIMALS LIKE COMPETING. USING THEM FOR SPORT IS NO WORSE THAN KILLING THEM FOR FOOD.

B *People disagree about whether or not animals should be used in sport*

Hunting

Survival of the first humans depended upon the skill of a hunter to bring food to his family and tribe. Once food became easier to get, hunting became a sport rather than a necessity. However, in some parts of the world, like the Arctic, people still need to hunt for food to survive. In Britain, most hunting is classed as a sport.

Supporters say it helps the countryside, for example, by removing pests like foxes, which attack livestock or wildlife and can spread disease. They think trapping or poisoning animals may be more cruel and less effective than hunting.

Opponents of hunting successfully argued that chasing and killing a fox with hounds is cruel. Parliament passed a law in 2004 banning hare coursing and the hunting of wild mammals with dogs.

Objectives

Consider the arguments for and against using animals in sport, in hunting and in bullfighting.

Understand religious attitudes to these issues.

A *Throughout history people have used animals in sport*

Activities

1. If animals are there for our use, is there anything wrong with using them in sport? Refer to the teachings of at least one religion in your answer.

2. Are trapping or poisoning better methods of killing foxes than hunting or shooting them?

⚭ links

Find out more at:
www.countryside-alliance.org.uk
www.league.org.uk

Research activity

Find out more about the arguments used for and against fox hunting, for example the views of the Countryside Alliance and the League Against Cruel Sports. Write down what you find out, and make a note of what you think would be the view of one religion on the arguments presented.

Bullfighting

Bullfighting, with its colourful pageantry and element of danger, is popular in Spain and Portugal. After performing various moves to distract and anger the bull, the matador thrusts a sword into the bull to kill it. Supporters say it is a proud tradition that should be respected; the bull will be killed anyway, so it does not matter how it is done. Opponents think it is cruel and degrading. The bulls are teased and have sharp spears stuck into their bodies until they collapse exhausted from their injuries.

C   *A bullfight*

Religious attitudes

Buddhism

For Buddhists, compassion and loving kindness should extend to all living things. Hunting, fishing and trapping animals is not in keeping with the Eightfold Path. Buddhists would consider these activities as tormenting and abusing living creatures, which scriptures forbid.

Christianity

Some Christians believe hunting is justified since God told humans to bring animals under their control. Other Christians say animals are part of God's creation and humans have a duty as stewards to protect them.

Hinduism

Hindus think hunting is cruel and unnecessary. All creatures are part of Brahman. Protecting animals is part of a Hindu's duty. Hindus should practise non-violence.

Islam

Islam teaches that animals have feelings and a reason for living. Animals may be hunted for food but not sport. Allah will hold people accountable if they kill an animal for no useful purpose.

Judaism

For Jews, humans are responsible for looking after animals as God made them rulers over creation. The Bible teaches care and concern for the needs of animals. Jews disapprove of hunting, even if it is done for a living.

Sikhism

Some of the Sikh gurus hunted, but most Sikhs today are against hunting for sport. They believe God will judge them on such actions. They think the decision about whether or not to hunt is a matter for someone's conscience.

> **AQA   Examiner's tip**
>
> You need to be able to explain whether using animals in all sports or only in some sports is morally acceptable and to give a religious viewpoint on these issues.

D   *Some Sikh gurus hunted with falcons*

Summary

You should now be able to explain different views about whether animals should be used in sport, hunted or used in bullfighting. You should be able to discuss religious attitudes to these issues.

1.9 The fur and ivory trades

■ Fur

For most of human history, particularly in cold climates, humans have used all sorts of animals for fur clothing to keep themselves warm. Some are well known, such as mink, fox or rabbit. Some might surprise you, such as seal, squirrel, and even cat and dog. If humans kill animals for food, and use their skins for leather goods, what is the problem with using their fur for coats?

The fur trade

Some people wrongly think that fur has come from an animal that was killed for its meat rather than just its fur. This is not so. Over 55 million animals are killed each year for the **fur trade**. Fur farms keep hundreds of wild animals in small, individual cages to save their fur from damage. This prevents them from living a natural life. Methods of slaughter, such as electrocution, sometimes leave the animals conscious while they are being skinned. Fur farming was made illegal in England and Wales in 2000 (2002 in Scotland).

After many years of being seen as wrong, wearing fur recently made a comeback at designer fashion shows. Supporters argue the fur trade is worth up to £500 million a year to the UK economy. Fur is a natural, renewable resource. The fur trade helps people who make their living by trapping and hunting. No endangered species are used. Some animals are taken to reduce their numbers. The British Fur Trade Association is introducing an 'origin assured' label to reassure customers that the fur comes from a country with rules about producing fur.

Objectives

Consider whether animals should be killed for their fur or ivory.

Apply understanding of religious teachings to these issues.

Key terms

Fur trade: the business of farming or hunting wild animals for their fur to be made into clothing.

Ivory trade: the sale of ivory from elephants' tusks, often illegally.

⚬⚬ links

Find out more about this point of view at **www.britishfur.co.uk**

A *Who looks best in mink fur, the model or the mink?*

◼ The ivory trade

Most people think it is wrong to kill elephants just to get the ivory in their tusks, but experts believe the **ivory trade** is flourishing. Conservation groups who monitor the trade say armed gangs of poachers kill elephants in Central Africa. The ivory from their tusks finds its way into shops in Nigeria, the Ivory Coast and Senegal. The amount of ivory found there in 2003 represented tusks of more than 760 elephants, yet there are probably no more than 563 elephants left in these countries. This showed that it was being imported from other places.

The ivory trade and the law

The legal position is complicated. In 1989, the United Nations (UN) made the ivory trade illegal everywhere. However, since then it has allowed some limited trading to go ahead. Recently the European Union has approved the sale of 108 tonnes of ivory to China where there is a huge demand. Although it is said to be taken only from animals that died or were killed because of overpopulation, opponents say that allowing some legal sales only encourages the poachers.

Some African countries have laws limiting the ivory trade. However, they allow them to be broken because of corruption, a lack of political will and the difficulties of enforcing the law. Armed groups in a number of countries are using profits from ivory to fund military operations, so the killing of elephants is funding war.

B

Warlords turn to ivory trade to fund slaughter of humans

Independent, *Monday 17 March 2008*

Summary

You should now be able to explain the arguments for and against allowing trade in fur and ivory. You should be able to discuss a religious viewpoint on each, using your knowledge of religious beliefs about animals.

Activities

1 Why do some people object to wearing fur?

2 Even if the fur trade is subject to rules, do you think it is right to farm wild animals?

3 Explain why some people think that the ivory trade should be made illegal everywhere.

4 Based on the religious beliefs and teachings you have studied, explain how a believer in one religion might view the fur trade or the ivory trade. Explain your reasons.

Research activity 🔍

Using the internet or a library, find out more about the beliefs and work of an organisation that campaigns against the trade in fur or ivory. Record your findings so that you can use them as an example in your examination. Some useful websites are noted in the Links below. Make a note of a religious view on these issues, too.

∞ links

Find out more at:
www.bornfree.org.uk
(search for 'ivory')
www.peta.org.uk
www.caft.org.uk

AQA *Examiner's tip*

Review religious teachings you have studied so far and try to form a judgement on the attitude a religion would take to these issues.

1.10 Animal experiments

Animal experiments

Animal experiments are when medical drugs are tested on animals before they can be sold to humans. New drugs are injected into animals to test their effects. Many useful vaccines against human and animal diseases have been developed this way. However, drugs do not always affect animals in the same way as humans. In 2006 Ryan Wilson, a volunteer in a drug trial, had to have all his fingers and toes amputated because he reacted so badly to a drug. It had been previously tested on animals with no ill effects.

Testing cosmetics and toiletries on animals is now against the law. In medical research, companies are using cheaper, quicker alternatives. These have reduced the number of animal experiments. Instead of live animals, they use computers or experiment on cells. The government inspects laboratories to ensure animal suffering is kept to a minimum.

> **Government reports 3 million animal experiments in 2007**

> **Drug test results in modern-day 'Elephant Man'**

A

Genetic modification (GM)

People have always bred farm animals to improve their health and get better quality meat. However, **genetic modification** means that animals have been genetically altered in a laboratory. This is so scientists can study how genes work, study the effects of genetic diseases and test new drugs. Pigs have been developed (with human DNA) to supply organs for human transplantation. They have not yet been used. An 'oncomouse' has been genetically modified to be born with cancer for research.

Cloning

Cloning is creating an organism that is the exact genetic copy of another. Scientists in Scotland cloned Tracy the sheep. She produced a protein in her milk that could treat lung diseases like cystic fibrosis. Although there are benefits, thousands of animal embryos are destroyed while trying to clone them. Believers worry that the main motive for cloning animals will be to make money. Human health and safety risks might be ignored.

B *Dolly the sheep was the clone of Tracy the sheep*

∞ links

Read more about GM animals at: **www.parliament.uk** (search for 'GM animals')

Research activities

1. Find out more about the case of Ryan Wilson. Some websites are suggested in the Links to get you started.

2. Do you think his experience supports arguments for or against testing on animals? Make a note of your findings and refer to them in preparation for the examination.

∞ links

www.channel4.com (search for 'drug trial went wrong' in news)
http://news.bbc.co.uk (search for 'Ryan Wilson')

Religious attitudes

Some religious people are against genetic modification and cloning of animals. They think scientists are 'playing God' and interfering with nature by artificially changing the structure of a living creature. Some believers oppose all animal experiments on grounds of cruelty. Others accept animal experiments if they help save human lives.

Buddhism

Buddhists oppose animal experiments. They believe that life is as precious to every animal as it is to humans. Since all forms of life are dependent on each other, they think care for other creatures will improve human life.

Christianity

Christians believe that animals and birds are valuable to God (see Luke 12:6), but most Christians accept limited testing on animals in order to find a cure for diseases.

Hinduism

Hindu deities appear as animals, reminding the worshipper of the qualities found in the animal world. Animals should not be harmed as they are part of the great wheel of samsara (the cycle of life, death and rebirth) and are helpful to humans.

Islam

Animals have had legal rights in Islam since the 13th century. Caging animals is forbidden but animals may be used to find cures for diseases if suffering is minimal. Allah has entrusted humans with maintaining the unity of his creation, its wildlife and the natural environment (Muslim Declaration at Assisi).

Judaism

Jews are taught not to blemish or injure animals or cause them distress. However, animal testing is allowed to help advance medical science. People should be kind to creatures (Deuteronomy 22:6).

Sikhism

Sikhs think human superiority should not be seen as an excuse to mistreat animals. The Guru Granth Sahib teaches that God is present in all living beings and has a purpose for them. However, Sikhs accept animal testing if suffering is kept to a minimum and it advances medical science.

C   *Scientists study how genes work to understand genetic diseases better*

Activities

1   Do you think that all animal experiments are cruel? Explain your answer.

2   'Cloning animals is trying to play God.' What do you think? Explain your opinion. Would religious people agree with your views on this and question 1?

3   'Genetic modification is no worse than breeding animals to improve their quality.' Do you agree? Give reasons for your answer, showing that you have thought about more than one point of view. Refer to religious arguments in your answer.

Summary

You should now be able to discuss the moral issues raised for believers by animal experiments, genetic modification of animals and cloning and be able to explain how believers apply religious teaching to these issues.

AQA   Examiner's tip

You need to be able to explain the key terms on page 26 and discuss the moral issues they raise for religious believers.

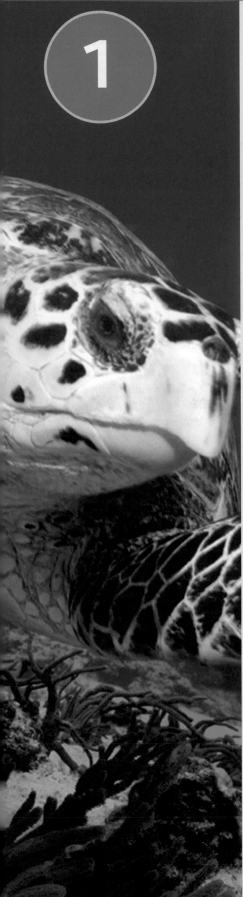

1

Religion and animal rights – summary

For the examination you should now be able to:

✔ explain the extent to which animals are different from humans and their relative values

✔ outline religious ideas about the status and rights of animals

✔ discuss the contemporary use and abuse of animals including:

– the treatment of wildlife and keeping animals in zoos

– using animals as companions, for transport or work

– using animals as food including free-range and factory farming

– issues concerning the slaughter of animals, meat, vegetarian and vegan diets

– using animals for sport including hunting and bullfighting

– using animals for profit, such as the fur and ivory trades

– using animals for experiments and the genetic modification and cloning of animals

✔ explain religious attitudes towards the use and abuse of animals

✔ explain religious views on the means of protecting animal rights and responses to preserving species from extinction.

Sample answer

1   Write an answer to the following examination question:

'It is wrong to keep animals in zoos.'

Do you agree? Give reasons for your answer, showing that you have thought about more than one point of view. Refer to religious arguments in your answer.

(6 marks)

2   Read the following sample answer.

> I do not agree with the statement. Zoos are brilliant. They can save rare species of animals as they help them breed and then put them back into the wild. Zoos teach children a lot about animals that they would never be able to see except on television. People study animals in zoos to learn more about animal life. Christians believe that God put humans in charge of his creation, therefore zoos are a good way of keeping wildlife alive.

3   Discuss with a partner. Do you think that there are other things that the student could have included in the answer?

4   What mark would you give this answer out of six? What are the reasons for the mark you have given? Look at the mark scheme in the Introduction on page 7 (AO2) to help you make a decision.

AQA Examination-style questions

1   Look at the newspaper headlines below and answer the following questions.

Factory farming provides cheap food

Ban the fur and ivory trades

Call to become vegetarians

(a) What is factory farming?   *(1 mark)*

(b) Give **two** reasons why many religious believers are against the fur and ivory trades.   *(2 marks)*

(c) 'Religious believers should be vegetarians.' What do you think? Explain
        your opinion.   *(3 marks)*

(d) Explain the attitudes of religious people to experiments on animals. Refer to
        religious teaching in your answer.   *(6 marks)*

(e) 'Animals are here for humans' benefit.' Do you agree? Give reasons for
        your answer, showing that you have thought about more than one point of view.
        Refer to religious arguments in your answer.   *(6 marks)*

> **AQA Examiner's tip** When asked if you agree with a statement, explain what you think, and why others might disagree. One-sided answers can only achieve four marks. Include religious arguments – without this, you can achieve only three marks.

2.1 The origins of life

■ A precious gift

Have you ever loaned a friend something that was precious to you, only to find that they damaged or destroyed it? Imagine how upset you would be if it was something that could not be replaced.

Many people think this sums up the way we treat the Earth. There is only one Earth and we cannot replace it. The way we live is damaging the planet, perhaps beyond repair. Most religions believe in creation – that the planet was made and given to us by God, and all believe that we should treat it with care. Religious beliefs about the origins of life (how life began) are sometimes expressed through creation stories. The main message of these is that God made the Earth for humans to use, not abuse.

Objectives

Introduce ideas about how people treat the Earth.

Explore religious beliefs about the origins of life.

> **Activity**
>
> 1 With a partner or in a small group, list 10 ways in which some people are damaging the planet. Share your findings with the class.

A There is only one Earth

■ Creation stories

Christianity and Judaism

Christians and Jews share creation stories written around 3,500 years ago. The Bible and the Torah begin with a story that tells how God created the heavens and the Earth out of nothing, filled the Earth with living creatures and made human beings (Genesis 1–2). God completed his work in six days and rested on the seventh day. The story does not explain how the planet came about. It says that it was already there but was covered in water and darkness. God made the planet able to support life (with plants and trees for food) and then made animals and humans.

A second story describes the creation of the first man and woman, Adam and Eve (Genesis 2:4–25). Although some Christians take these stories literally, most prefer to concentrate on the religious truths they teach about caring for the Earth rather than on their details, and believe that they were not written as scientific explanations for the origins of life.

Islam

The Qur'an teaches that Allah made the heavens and the Earth in six days (Surah 11:7). Man was created first, then woman, and all humans are descended from these two people (Surah 4:1). The Qur'an has a story that is similar to the story of Adam and Eve (Surah 2:31–37).

B A stained-glass window depicting the story of Adam and Eve

Hinduism

There are many Hindu stories about the activities of the gods who were involved in creation. In one, the god Vishnu was asleep on a cobra snake as it floated on the ocean. A humming sound awakened Vishnu and a lotus flower grew from his belly. Brahma, the creator, was sitting in the lotus flower and on Vishnu's command divided the flower into three parts to make the heavens, the Earth and the sky. He then made the grass, trees, flowers, animals, birds, fish and finally people.

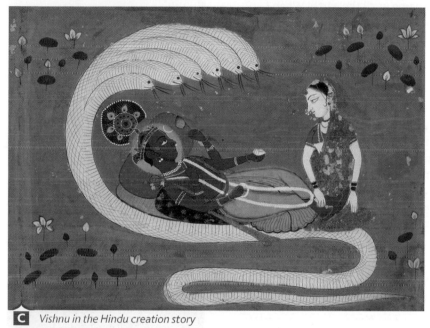

C   *Vishnu in the Hindu creation story*

Discussion activity

With a partner or in a small group, discuss the following statement, giving your reasons and making sure you think of more than one point of view. You might consider whether science has made religious stories pointless, or whether people misunderstand creation stories and treat them as science when they are not.

'Religious creation stories are no longer relevant today.'

Buddhism

There is no Buddhist creation story. The Buddha thought questions about how the Earth started were idle speculation. No answer would satisfy everyone. Buddhists believe that worlds evolve and follow a cycle of decay, death and rebirth.

Sikhism

There is no specific Sikh creation story. Sikhs believe that God created the Earth because he wanted to, as an act of love. Only God knows all the secrets of creation because human knowledge is limited, but people can find evidence of God in the natural world.

Activity

2   Explain in writing one religion's beliefs about the creation of the Earth.

AQA   *Examiner's tip*

Try to learn a creation story so that you can support your answer with a specific example in the examination if you are asked a question on this area.

AQA   *Examiner's tip*

Remember that Buddhists do not believe in a being called God, so they do not think God created the universe.

Summary

You should now be able to explain religious beliefs about the origins of life and to discuss how believers might apply these beliefs to looking after the world.

The 'wow' factor

Oh Lord, our Lord, how majestic is your name in all the earth! When I consider your heavens, the work of your fingers, the moon and the stars which you have set in place, what is man that you are mindful of him, the son of man that you care for him?

Psalms 8:1, 3–4

Science reveals a world filled with mystery, **awe** and **wonder**, which inspires people to investigate things and think about the purpose of life on earth. Even non-religious scientists have a sense of reverence or respect for the natural world that makes them devote their lives to its study.

> *Scientists can sense the vastness of even the smallest things. They know that these things have unending connections with the rest of life… And most great scientists have named awe of this kind as their deepest reason for pursuing science at all.*
>
> Mary Midgeley, 'The Need for Wonder' in God for the 21st Century

> *One cannot help but be in awe when he contemplates the mysteries of eternity, of life, of the marvellous structure of reality.*
>
> Albert Einstein, quoted by Michael Reagan in The Hand of God

The popularity of wildlife television programmes suggests that people are fascinated by the way nature works. Children watch the hatching of chicks or the birth of kittens in wonder and delight. New parents often say the birth of a child made them feel awe and wonder at the miracle of new life. Without a sense of awe and wonder at the mysteries of nature or its power and beauty, our lives can remain flat and boring.

Some people worry that humans have lost their sense of awe and wonder and take the planet for granted. Science has explained many of the mysteries of life and the universe, so perhaps people do not feel a sense of reverence for its wonders. One Jewish thinker, Rabbi Heschel, stated that humanity will perish from a lack of appreciation of the world rather than a lack of understanding of it.

Explore relgious and other views about the nature of planet Earth (e.g. awe and wonder).

Awe: a feeling of respect; insight into meaning greater than oneself.

Wonder: marvelling at the complexity and beauty of the universe.

A   The complexity and beauty of the universe

1   Have you ever experienced awe and wonder? Share your thoughts with a partner or in a small group.

2   Have some people lost the ability to be amazed and delighted at nature or the universe? Explain your opinion.

3   What effects might taking the planet for granted have on its future?

Religious responses

Religions use the idea of the sanctity of life to express their belief that life is precious because it was given by God. (Buddhists believe life is precious, but do not believe in a Creator God.)

Buddhism

To Buddhists, the universe is a single, vast living thing. All parts of the natural world depend on each other. Since humans are part of nature they should not act against it.

Christianity

Christians believe God created the universe as an expression of his love. As God's children, humans have the **responsibility** to care for and protect the natural world and be thankful to God for his gift.

Hinduism

Hindus believe the world is sacred and precious because everything in the universe comes from God and is part of God. Reverence for the whole of creation is the proper human response. Hindus believe that the Earth is our mother and we are her children.

Islam

For Muslims, the universe was created by Allah and belongs to him, not to humans. God's oneness or unity is reflected in the oneness of humans with nature. People must care for the world for future generations.

Judaism

Jews believe in the goodness of God's creation (as shown in the quotation at the start of this section) and say prayers of thanksgiving for the continual daily miracle of existence. They believe that humans have a responsibility to defend nature against exploitation and abuse.

Sikhism

For Sikhs, the complexity and order of creation shows what God is like. Everything in nature is connected for survival. Sikhs think many people misunderstand the universe, thinking it exists on its own, whereas it really exists because God wills it to exist.

B *Religions accept the use, not the abuse, of the Earth's resources*

 links

For more on the idea of the sanctity of life, see pages 10–11, 74–75, 98–99 and the Glossary.

Key terms

Responsibility: duty; the idea that we are in charge of our own actions.

Discussion activity ●●●

Do you agree with Rabbi Heschel's comment, stated on the previous page, that a lack of appreciation of the world threatened humanity? Explain your opinions and make notes.

AQA Examiner's tip

Make sure you can explain 'awe' and 'wonder' and discuss religious attitudes to planet Earth when you are asked about this in the examination.

Summary

You should now be able to explain what it means to respond to the natural world with awe and wonder and explain religious views about the nature of planet Earth.

2.3 Caring for planet Earth

Religious ideas

Most religions, through their creation stories or other teachings, believe that:

- God created the Earth with the right conditions to sustain life
- God created all living things, including people
- the world really belongs to God, not to human beings
- plants, fish, birds and animals were created for people to use and to make the Earth a beautiful place to live
- God deliberately made living things capable of reproducing naturally, so nature continues God's work in the creation of new life.

Stewardship

The religious idea that people have been given a special responsibility to be in charge of the Earth, to protect and care for it, is called **stewardship**. Since the Earth belongs to God, people have a duty as stewards to look after it on God's behalf. In return, we are able to use what the Earth provides for our own survival. People do not have a right to abuse the natural world.

Religious people believe that God will judge humans when they die on how well they look after the Earth. They think that respecting God by looking after his creation will help to ensure a good afterlife. Those who believe in reincarnation believe they will return to Earth, so will want to ensure they have a good Earth to return to.

Caring for the Earth

Buddhism

The Dhammapada teaches Buddhists not to do evil, but rather to do good. Buddhists should develop an attitude of loving kindness to all things, including the Earth. Humans may use nature to make useful things, but must not exploit it unnecessarily. Just as the bee takes nectar without destroying a flower, so humans should take what they need without damaging the universe.

Christianity

In the past, the instruction by God to 'rule over … every living creature' was understood in terms of domination rather than stewardship. Now Christians believe they have a duty to conserve the Earth for future generations.

Hinduism

Hindus believe that everything in the universe comes from God (Brahman) and is part of God. It is important to show reverence for the whole of creation. The world is sacred and must be cared for. People's wellbeing depends on right attitudes to the Earth and its resources.

Objectives

Understand the concept of stewardship.

Understand religious beliefs about care and responsibility for the planet.

AQA *Examiner's tip*

Remember that Buddhists do not believe in a being called God, so do not think God created the universe. However, they insist that the Earth should be cared for and no living thing should be harmed.

Key terms

Stewardship: the idea that believers have a duty to look after the environment on behalf of God.

A *Stewardship means that people can use the Earth for producing food, if they look after it*

∞ links

Look at the teachings regarding animals given in Chapter 1. Many are also relevant to caring for the Earth.

Islam

Muslims believe the world belongs to its Creator Allah who appointed humans as trustees over it. To abuse that God-given authority is insulting God. Humans will be answerable to Allah on the Day of Judgement for their use or misuse of the Earth's resources. Creation is like God's family – God loves the most those who are kindest to his family.

Judaism

God placed Adam in the Garden of Eden to farm it and look after it (stewardship). The Torah teaches that the land should not be over-exploited and should be shared. Other passages guide Jews on responsible stewardship.

Sikhism

The world belongs to God, the creator who dwells in all things. Humans are part of nature and their wellbeing is connected to it. It is a God-given duty to conserve and protect the Earth.

B   *All of nature depends on every other part: bees pollinate plants that humans need for food*

Research activity

Using the internet or a library, find some relevant teachings from the religions you are studying. Look for sacred texts and/or contemporary leaders' statements about the responsibility humans have to the care of the planet. For example, look up the websites in the Link box for Pope Benedict's speech for the celebration of the World Day of Peace, or the Dalai Lama's words about the environment. Use a search engine to find other examples. Make a note of these texts or statements and revise them for use in the examination.

links

Find out more at:

www.vatican.va (search for 'world peace 2008')

http://hhdl.dharmakara.net (click on 'The Dalai Lama on the Environment')

Discussion activity

1   With a partner or in a small group, discuss the following statements. Make sure you think about more than one point of view, using the prompts given, and give reasons for your opinions.

a   'The world belongs to God, so let God take care of it.' Do people or God have responsibility for the planet? What do you think?

b   'People who do not believe in God do not need to take care of the planet.' Are non-believers less likely to care for the planet than believers? Do believers have more responsibility for the planet precisely because of their beliefs? What do you think?

Activity

Explain three practical ways you think religious people might carry out their role as 'stewards'. Are religious people doing enough?

Summary

You should now be able to explain the meaning of 'stewardship' and religious beliefs about the care of and responsibility for the planet.

AQA   Examiner's tip

You need to be able to discuss the beliefs and teachings of at least one religion about care and responsibility for the planet when answering a question on this topic.

Effects of modern lifestyles

The way we live now

The Earth is the only planet with an environment and resources that can support human life. If people destroy the planet, they will destroy themselves in the process. Modern life is putting more strains on the planet than ever before. Some threats to the environment include:

- **carbon emissions** from vehicles, power stations and factories
- greenhouse gases destroying the ozone layer
- increasing amounts of waste
- pollution of rivers and seas by oil, pesticides and nitrates
- deforestation and destruction of natural habitats
- using up natural resources faster than they can be replaced.

These problems will be considered in more detail below and throughout this chapter.

A *Global warming causes the polar icecap to melt, destroying the polar bear's natural habitat*

The greenhouse effect and global warming

Pollution is created by emissions of gases from cars, power stations and factories that burn fuels like coal, oil, and gas. These gases cover the earth like a blanket. They trap the sun's heat, like the glass in a greenhouse. Most people agree that this **greenhouse effect** causes global warming or climate change. Sea levels rise as the icecaps of Earth's highest mountains and the polar icecap melt. Low-lying coastlines will gradually disappear under rising water levels. Some scientists debate whether or not this is caused by humans.

Emissions from cars and factories

Britain's roads are full of traffic. Carbon monoxide from vehicles causes smog in major cities, making it difficult to breathe. Cars also produce carbon dioxide (CO_2), one of the greenhouse gases that contribute to climate change.

Factories release a chemical mix into the air that travels across borders, falling as acid rain. Factories also heat their buildings and use vehicles to transport goods, adding to their carbon emissions. With the increase in industrial activity in all parts of the world, some think the levels of CO_2 and other chemicals in the atmosphere will double in less than a century. This is despite many nations' promises to cut emissions.

Objectives

Explore what effects modern lifestyles have on the planet, such as emissions from cars, factories and waste.

Consider responses to these problems, such as recycling.

⚭ links

To apply religious teachings on stewardship and caring for the Earth to these issues, see pages 34–35 and the Glossary.

Key terms

Carbon emissions: release of greenhouse gases, such as carbon monoxide from vehicles, into the atmosphere.

Greenhouse effect: the trapping of heat from the sun in the lower atmosphere due to an increase in carbon dioxide, methane and other pollution.

Recycling: reusing old products to make new ones.

⚭ links

See pages 44–45 for more about the debate on global warming and climate change.

B *Emissions from factories pollute the Earth*

⚭ links

For more about acid rain see pages 38–39.

Waste

Household waste

Some people say we are a 'throwaway society'. Everything, including food waste, packaging, household appliances, furniture and electronic equipment, goes to the tip and much of it is not biodegradable (able to be broken down by bacteria in the environment). However, people are starting to realise that things like glass and paper can be reused, saving money and the environment.

Industrial waste

Industrial waste is even harder to deal with because it may contain dangerous chemicals that take a long time to disappear. These can affect human health and the natural habitat. Waste from nuclear power stations is particularly dangerous because its radioactivity lasts for thousands of years and can seep into soil and drinking water, causing cancer and illness in people who live nearby.

Recycling

People are now more aware of the importance of recycling in saving money, resources and the environment. Most households now recycle glass, cans, newspapers, cardboard, plastic and garden waste.

Recycling helps save the environment by:

- saving energy, which reduces carbon emissions. For example, making new paper from old paper uses 60 per cent less energy than making new paper from trees
- conserving natural resources so protecting natural habitats
- reducing the need for landfill sites (rubbish tips) that produce methane, a greenhouse gas.

Activities

1. Explain how the greenhouse effect and global warming might affect planet Earth. How does this fit with teachings on stewardship?

2. How does your school or college try to help the environment? Is there anything further you could do?

3. Only 9 per cent of waste is from households. Most is from industry. Are household recycling schemes a waste of time?

4. Read the case study. If the government improves public transport, will people cut back on using cars? What do you think? Explain your opinion.

AQA Examiner's tip

In considering these issues, make sure you think about what religious people would say about them, based on your knowledge of the religious beliefs and teachings given throughout this book.

Case study

'Traffic hell' predicted with 6m more cars by 2031

Britain will descend into 'traffic hell' with nearly six million more cars running on British roads by 2031, an environmental group has warned. The Campaign for Better Transport urged the government to cut car use by improving rail and bus services and making public transport cheaper. The group's director said, 'We can't go on like this. Traffic is destroying our communities, our health and our environment.'

© adapted from Dan Milmo, transport correspondent the Guardian, Monday September 10 2007

C

AQA Examiner's tip

It is helpful to learn and use the correct key terms in your answers about environmental problems. Use the definitions throughout the chapter and in the glossary to help you.

Summary

You should now be able to explain key terms, discuss some effects of modern lifestyles on the planet including emissions from cars, factories and waste. You should be able to explain recycling and why it is important.

2.5 Pollution

Introduction

Pollution means the contamination of something, especially the environment. Pollution spoils or causes harm to nature by poisoning the environment.

Acid rain

Some gas emissions from cars, factories and power stations combine with water vapour in the air to make acids, which may end up in rainwater. This is known as **acid rain**. Acid rain poisons lakes and rivers, the soil, plants and trees, especially those that receive doses over a long period of time. Forests and fish all over the world are dying because acid rain can be carried great distances in the atmosphere. It also damages buildings.

A *This forest has been destroyed by acid rain*

Oil spills

The huge demand for oil means that tankers carry crude oil to all parts of the world. Ships can get into trouble, hit rocks and cause **oil spills**. This can ruin coastlines and cover seabirds and marine life in a thick, toxic (poisonous) coating. Most oil pollution in the sea is said to be from industries on land. However, public attention is usually focussed on dramatic pictures of shipwrecks like the Exxon Valdez (1989), which had long-lasting effects on Alaskan wildlife. The oil damages seabirds' feathers so they are less buoyant, unable to fly well to hunt for food and vulnerable to cold and infection. Without human help, they die. The coats of seals and sea otters also lose insulation so they can die of cold, or they eat fish affected by the spill and are poisoned.

Objectives

Explore the problems caused by pollution, including acid rain, oil spills, toxic chemicals, and pesticides.

Understand religious and other responses to the issue of pollution.

⚭ links

For more on emissions see pages 36–37.

Key terms

Pollution: the contamination of something, especially the environment.

Acid rain: rain made acid by contamination through pollution in the atmosphere as the result of emissions from factories, vehicles, power stations, and so on.

Oil spills: leaking of oil into the environment, usually the sea.

Toxic chemicals: poisonous chemicals.

Pesticides: substances (poison) used to destroy insects and pests that attack crops.

⚭ links

To apply religious teachings on stewardship and caring for the Earth to these issues, see pages 34–35 and the Glossary.

B *Cleaning-up after an oil spill is costly and dirty work*

Toxic chemicals

The world's chemical industries produce thousands of chemicals each year. Environmental groups say they do not test the chemicals enough or consider their impact on the environment. People buy so many pieces of electronic equipment that contain **toxic chemicals** that it is difficult to dispose of them safely. Breaking up old ships creates toxic waste, so developed countries often transfer this dirty job to developing countries, exporting the environmental damage to others.

Pesticides

Pesticides are poisonous substances that control weeds, pests and diseases. Farmers spray their crops with them to get the best yield. Pesticides are a serious hazard to wildlife. At high doses they not only kill insects but birds and mammals as well. They seep down into the soil and get into the water table. They are also absorbed into the atmosphere where they fall to Earth as acid rain. The law controls the use of pesticides in Britain but some campaigners think it does not do enough to protect public health and the environment.

The world's worst chemical disaster took place in Bhopal, India in 1984. Toxic gas leaked from a poorly maintained pesticide plant, killing up to 20 thousand people and leaving 120 thousand permanently ill. The polluted site of the abandoned factory still leaks poison into local water supplies.

What does religion say?

Pollution is a fairly recent problem so the founders of the world's religions did not speak about it. However, their teachings can be applied to the issues. Polluting the planet is not good stewardship, as God's creation is being abused. Pollution harms people so is not following Christian teaching to 'love one's neighbour'. It harms living creatures so is against the Buddhist first precept not to harm living beings.

Activity

Choose one of the following: acid rain, oil spills, toxic chemicals or pesticides. With a partner, explain how the one you have chosen affects the environment.

Then join with others who have studied a different cause of pollution and share your information. Make a presentation of your findings to the class.

Research activity

Using the internet or a library, find out what Greenpeace, Friends of the Earth, Christian Aid or the World Wide Fund for Nature (WWF) say about pollution and the use of toxic chemicals and pesticides. Record their statements or arguments in a fact file. You can revise these examples to use in the examination. Using your answers to Discussion activities 1 and 2 discuss whether the information you have found changes or strengthens your opinion on what can be done to stop pollution. Make notes on key points that you can refer to in preparation for the examination.

AQA Examiner's tip

Be sure you are able to understand and explain the key terms on page 38, and relate the issues to religious teachings on stewardship.

links

Find out more at:

www.greenpeace.org.uk
www.foe.co.uk
www.christianaid.org.uk
www.wwf.org.uk

Discussion activities

1 With a partner, in a small group or as a class, discuss what you think can be done to stop the environmental problems mentioned on these pages.

2 'There is nothing one person alone can do to protect the natural world.' What do you think? Explain your opinion. Do you think religious people have a special responsibility? Refer to teachings on stewardship in your discussion, and make a note of key points to refer to in your revision.

Summary

You should now be able to explain the problems caused by pollution, including acid rain, oil spills, toxic chemicals and pesticides and discuss religious and other responses to the issues.

Natural habitats destruction

Every 20 minutes the world loses at least one species of animal or plant life. Around 27,000 species each year are becoming extinct. The concern for the preservation of animals, fish and plants is a major issue. Yet as human populations grow, bigger cities are created. Providing the resources needed to support people in them results in the destruction of **natural habitats**. Britain has also seen the loss of birds, insects and animals through changing farming methods, the use of pesticides, industrial pollution and the building of houses and roads.

Tropical rainforests are disappearing at an alarming rate, with over one and a half million square kilometres cut down in the last 10 years. Rainforests contain more than half of all species on our planet. Some creatures live so deep in the forests they have not even been discovered yet. If the forests are destroyed these species will become extinct.

National parks have been created to protect and preserve the natural habitat of many species, but these may not be enough to save the great variety of living creatures.

Deforestation

Deforestation is the permanent destruction of native forests and woodlands. It is usually done to:

- clear the land for farming to feed rising populations
- raise cattle for beef
- raise crops that can be sold abroad
- cut trees like mahogany and teak for furniture
- cut trees like oak and pine for building and firewood.

Effects of deforestation

- Deforestation destroys the natural habitats of animals and plants so that they face extinction.
- Deforestation contributes to climate change. Trees take up CO_2 from the atmosphere in order to live. When forests are cleared, trees are burned or rot, so they release CO_2 into the atmosphere, making a major contribution to the greenhouse effect.
- Trees also draw water up through their roots and release it into the atmosphere, from where it falls back to Earth as rain. In the Amazon rainforests, over half the water circulating remains within the plants. When trees are removed, the region cannot hold as much water, which can result in a drier climate.
- With the loss of protective cover from trees, soil washes away into water courses, lakes and dams. This can cause flooding and landslides.

The problem of deforestation is made worse because the poor soils of tropical areas do not support farming for very long, so people move on and clear more forests. An area of forest equal to 20 football or rugby pitches is lost every minute.

Objectives

Explore the different ways in which the natural habitats of creatures are being destroyed, including by deforestation.

Key terms

Natural habitats: the places where species of plants or animals live in the wild.

Deforestation: the cutting down of large amounts of forest, usually because of business needs.

A *This kind of lush tropical rainforest is fast disappearing*

∞ links

For information on the greenhouse effect see pages 36–37 and the Glossary.

B *The gorilla is one of many animals facing extinction because of deforestation*

Religion	Teaching
Buddhism	Monks and nuns may not 'destroy any plant or tree'. (Vinaya Pitaka)
Christianity	'The Earth and all life on it are … given to us to share and develop, not to dominate and exploit.' (Roman Catholic Church, 1991)
Hinduism	'The Earth has enough for everyone's need, not everyone's greed.' (Mahatma Gandhi)
Islam	'There is no altering the laws of Allah's creation.' (Surah 30.30)
Judaism	'Do not destroy … trees by putting an axe to them, because you can eat their fruit.' (Deuteronomy 20:19)
Sikhism	'God prevails in all his creation … he continues to give us our daily bread which never fails.' (Guru Granth Sahib)

C   *Religious teachings on loss of habitats*

D   *Deforestation*

Research activity

Using the internet or a library, find out more about the loss of natural habitat in Britain, particularly in your local area. The sites listed in the Links may help you. What are the causes of the loss of insect, bird, animal or plant life in the UK? What is being done about it? Make notes on key points and revise them so that you can use them in the examination.

links

Find out more at:

http://greenfinder.co.uk (click on 'local groups and projects')

http://community.foe.co.uk (click on 'biodiversity')

Activities

1   With a partner or in a small group, list and explain why natural habitats are under threat in Britain.

2   Explain why you think people in developing countries clear forests.

3   Choose one religion's teachings about the environment and explain how a believer in that religion might apply those teachings to the issues discussed on these pages.

Extension activity

Working with a partner, think up some ways in which the effects of deforestation could be lessened. Make notes, and then add a note on how the ways you have discussed would support religious teachings on loss of habitats.

Discussion activity

1   With a partner or in a small group, discuss the following statements. Try to think of different points of view and also what religious people might say about the issue. Make notes on key points and revise them so that you can use them in the examination.

a   'Deforestation would stop if everyone became vegetarian.'

b   'Humans need homes more than animals.'

Summary

You should now be able to explain the why the destruction of natural habitat, including deforestation, is a matter of concern and be able to apply religious teachings to the issues.

The population explosion

- The world's population is increasing by 3,500 people every 20 minutes.
- It took all of recorded history until 1830 for the world population to reach one billion.
- Since 1830, population growth has 'exploded'.

The population explosion is stretching the Earth's natural resources to the limit. Some threats to the environment caused by the way we live are covered on pages 36 and 37. No one can blame humans for supporting themselves and their families. The question is whether we are blindly and greedily using up far too many resources without thinking of the long-term good of the planet.

Non-renewable natural resources

Oil, coal and gas

Fossil fuels like oil, coal and gas are called non-renewable resources because they cannot be replaced. They are used to produce electricity, which, once it is used, cannot be renewed. Yet humans use large amounts of these energy sources, sometimes wastefully.

The world will soon run out of oil and non-renewable sources of energy. None will be left for future generations. The amount of these fuels used by motorised transport is increasing. More people take flights abroad and have more than one car per family.

B *The electricity lighting this city at night is non-renewable*

Metals

Industry uses vast quantities of metals and little gets recycled. Many elements will run out before the end of the century. As they become rarer, their price will go up. People may breed endangered species of animals, but the basic chemical elements of the Earth cannot be replaced once they are gone.

Objectives

Understand why natural resources are under pressure.

Explore the use and abuse of natural resources, such as oil.

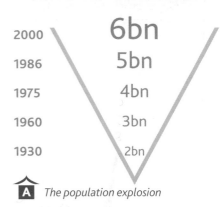

2000	6bn
1986	5bn
1975	4bn
1960	3bn
1930	2bn

A *The population explosion*

AQA Examiner's tip

You will not be asked about the world population explosion in the examination, but you can use it as one reason for the increased demands humans are placing on the natural resources of the Earth.

Element	Use
Gallium, indium	Liquid crystal displays on flat-screen televisions.
Hafnium	Computer chips and control rods for nuclear reactors.
Zinc	Cars and computers.
Copper	Water pipes and electrical wires.

C *Uses of elements – these elements will all run out by 2099*

Renewable energy sources

Scientists are working on the use of alternative renewable energies such as wind, wave and solar power. Cars are being developed that use hydrogen or other renewable fuels. Wind farms have sprung up around the country and off the coasts in the North Sea, for example. However, many people have objected that wind farms spoil the look of the countryside. Wave power needs further development and may not be cost effective.

Nuclear power

The UK government supports a new generation of nuclear power stations to provide a secure energy supply and to help tackle climate change. Nuclear power is cleaner than burning fossil fuels but the waste remains radioactive (giving off dangerous radiation) for thousands of years. An accident or terrorist attack on a nuclear plant would be disastrous. Environmental groups argue that nuclear plants will not cut emissions by the necessary amount and are highly dangerous. They think the government should invest in safer sources of renewable energy.

D   *Alternatives to fossil fuels are not always popular*

Religious attitudes

Many individual religious believers probably waste resources as much as anyone else. However, religious teachings make it clear that the Earth belongs to God. Humans have a duty to care not only for the planet but also for their fellow human beings. This makes some issues complicated because the welfare of people must be weighed against the welfare of the planet in years to come. Religions see both going hand in hand to conserve the world and its peoples.

links

See the religious teachings related to these issues on pages 30–35.

Summary

You should now be able to explain the use and abuse of natural resources and discuss the issues they raise for the future of the planet.

2.8 Climate change

The debate about climate change

In recent years scientists have argued about the causes of **climate change**. While some were urging governments to reduce greenhouse gas emissions, others were saying there was no evidence that humans were affecting climate change. These scientists argued that the Earth's climate is always changing, and that predictions about future **global warming** are unreliable and alarmist. Many industries, particularly the oil industry, support these views. Changing their production methods to cut greenhouse gas emissions would cost them a huge amount of money.

There is now a high level of agreement that average global temperatures have been rising for at least a century. The amount of CO_2 in the atmosphere has increased by 33 per cent since the Industrial Revolution in 19th-century Europe. Greenhouse gases are trapping more of the sun's energy, so the warming of the planet is evident. Most scientists think it is important for nations to take urgent steps to cut greenhouse gas emissions to reduce global warming. They also believe countries need to prepare for its serious but manageable impact on the Earth.

Research activity

1 The Royal Society is the UK's independent academy of science. Its website (www.royalsociety.org) will give you more information on the debate about climate change, from the UK's top scientists. Visit the site and make notes on key points that you can use in the examination.

Effects of global warming

Most scientists warn that global warming will result in severe weather leading to **droughts** or floods. These in turn cause the destruction of food crops leading to **famine**. Global warming could make water scarce, damaging agriculture, health, forests, plants and animals. Low-lying countries, such as Bangladesh, will be worst affected by flooding. The poorest people in the world, who already have fresh water shortages and inadequate healthcare, will suffer most from contaminated water and disease.

However, some scientists disagree. They say that extreme weather, for example, hurricanes in the Atlantic, are not definitely linked to global warming. They also say that there is not sufficient proof that global warming is the cause of the rapidly melting icecap on Africa's Mount Kilimanjaro or the collapse of an Antarctic ice shelf. However, more scientific studies are being published all the time. Many people now feel that there is enough evidence to start taking action, even if conclusive proof of certain connections is not yet available.

Objectives

Consider the debate about climate change and global warming.

Consider the effects of global warming, such as severe weather, droughts, floods, famine, destruction of crops, and the effects on plants and animals.

Think about religious attitudes to climate change.

∞ links

Read more about the greenhouse effect and global warming on pages 36–37 and 40–41.

Key terms

Climate change: the idea that the climate is getting warmer (global warming).

Global warming: the scientific concept that the world is getting warmer.

Droughts: long periods of abnormally low rainfall.

Famine: starvation owing to drastic, far-reaching food shortage.

A *A melting ice shelf*

B   *Severe weather, flooding and drought may all worsen through global warming*

Case study

Global warming and developing countries

Scientists predict that as global temperatures rise, sea levels will rise, partly owing to the melting of polar icecaps and snow on the world's highest mountains. A 1m rise in sea levels could flood 17 per cent of Bangladesh, where tens of millions of people now live. This would greatly affect their rice-growing capacity. The cost of rice would rise as production is lost. Fresh water supplies would be scarce and diseases associated with floods and drought, such as diarrhoea, would lower life expectancy. People and animals would have to flee their homes and move to neighbouring countries. In countries in Africa where it is already hot and desert-like, higher temperatures could mean complete loss of agricultural land to the desert and greater starvation than already present.

AQA   *Examiner's tip*

Make sure you are able to give a religious viewpoint on these issues from your knowledge of religious beliefs and teachings.

Religious attitudes

Most religious believers consider climate change an important issue because of the harm it can do to people, animals and the delicately balanced system of life on Earth. Many would also see the exploitation and abuse of the Earth's resources as a sign of sinfulness and greed. Religious principles of good stewardship, sanctity of life, love of neighbour, compassion for the poor, living in harmony with the natural world are applied to environmental problems by all religions.

∞ links

You can find out more about how religions have applied their beliefs and teachings to environmental problems on pages 48–49.

Activity

1   With a partner, in a small group or as a class, answer the following questions.

a   Outline the reasons why some scientists do not accept climate change.

b   Read the case study that describes some effects on developing countries. Do you think the developed world has a responsibility to help other countries, or is it just somebody else's problem? Do you think religious teachings give believers a special responsibility?

c   Are there any benefits to global warming? Explain your opinions.

Summary

You should now be able to explain the debate about and effects of climate change, including severe weather, droughts, floods, famine, destruction of crops, on plants and animals and give a religious view on these issues.

■ Religious responses

Religious beliefs in stewardship, responsibility for the Earth and concern about inequality of resources have prompted religious leaders and believers to join in campaigning for conservation and sustainable development.

⚭ links

See pages 30–35 for more about these religious beliefs.

■ Conservation

Conservation is looking after the environment and protecting animals. There are groups devoted to conserving everything from butterflies to the great apes, from the polar icecaps to local parks. Councils encourage people to be 'green' by recycling, buying organic food (on which no pesticides or artificial fertilisers are used), and finding alternatives to using a car. Environmental pressure groups educate, campaign and protest about activities that damage the planet.

⚭ links

Read more about environmental pressure groups on pages 14–15.

■ Earth Summits

An **Earth Summit** is a meeting of representatives of different countries, including religious leaders. They discuss the threat to the Earth and agree on international action. There have been three Earth Summits, as listed below.

Rio de Janeiro 1992

The first Earth Summit discussed pollution, deforestation and the growing scarcity of water. The Summit produced Agenda 21, a plan for saving the planet in the 21st century. The plan urged countries to find alternative sources of energy, to protect animal and plant species and to promote **sustainable development**. Countries also agreed to keep greenhouse gas emissions at a steady level.

Kyoto 1997

The Kyoto Protocol was agreed at this meeting. Countries promised to cut their CO_2 and other greenhouse gas emissions. If they merely maintained or actually increased their emissions, they agreed to carbon trading – paying another country with low emissions to offset their own.

Johannesburg 2002

The World Summit on Sustainable Development discussed the problems of the poor, particularly the two billion people who live without clean water. The Summit was also concerned about the loss of many animal and plant species, and the reduced numbers of fish in the sea. The 185 countries that attended agreed to work hard to combat these problems by 2015.

Objectives

Explore the work being done to look after the world, including conservation, Earth Summits, international action, targets to reduce carbon emissions or greenhouse gases, and sustainable development.

Understand that religious leaders and believers have joined with others in promoting conservation.

Key terms

Conservation: looking after the environment and protecting animals.

Earth Summits: informal name for United Nations Conferences on Environment and Development.

Sustainable development: development which takes into consideration the impact on the natural world for future generations.

A *Earth summits try to protect animal and plant species*

⚭ links

Find out more about this Summit at:

www.guardian.co.uk (search the environment section for 'Johannesburg Earth Summit' and click on the article 'Earth Summit')

Targets to reduce carbon emissions

After agreeing to cut carbon emissions at the Earth Summits, governments had to put their promises into action. The British government published a draft Climate Change Bill in March 2007. This promised a 60 per cent cut (from 1990 levels) in carbon emissions by 2050 and a 26 to 32 per cent reduction by 2020. The Bill is legally binding. These are challenging targets that some say will not be achieved at the current level of effort.

Sustainable development

> Development which meets the needs of the present without compromising the ability of future generations to meet their own needs.
>
> *UK government definition of sustainable development*

Our present way of life is placing increasing burdens on the planet. This is unsustainable – it cannot go on. The world's population continues to increase and already over a billion people live on less than a dollar a day. At the current rate, the world's water will run out in three decades. Already some two million children under five die every year from drinking dirty water.

Research activity

Using the internet or a library, research conservation projects, such as Kew Gardens, the World Land Trust or the Eden Project. Record your findings on at least one project and refer to them in preparation for your examination. You might also ask a member of a local faith community whether they support particular 'green' projects, and add any information they give you to your findings.

Discussion activity

1   With a partner or in a small group, discuss the following. Consider both sides of the issues, including religious arguments. Make notes on key points and revise them so that you can use them in the examination.

a   'Rich countries have no right to tell poor countries to stop their carbon emissions.'

b   'Earth Summits are all talk and no action.'

Summary

You should now be able to describe the work being done to look after the world both locally and through international action and discuss the importance of sustainable development.

AQA Examiner's tip

Review religious teachings you have studied earlier in this chapter and try to form a judgement on the attitude a religion would take to these issues.

Extension activity

Calculate your own 'carbon footprint'. You can work it out at the ACT ON CO2 website (http://campaigns.direct.gov.uk (search for 'ACT ON CO2' and click on the link)). You may be able to use the information as an example in the examination.

links

Read more about sustainable development at:

www.defra.gov.uk (click on 'Sustainable development' and then 'UK Government')

B   *Kew Gardens*

links

Find out more at:

www.kew.org (click on 'Conservation & wildlife')

www.worldlandtrust.org (click on 'Projects')

www.edenproject.com

Religious leaders and the environment

World religious leaders met at Assisi (1986) and Ohito (1995) to discuss environmental problems. Following are some of the key points made at Assisi.

Buddhism

Destruction of the environment is a result of greed, ignorance and disregard for the richness of all living things. If it continues, future generations will inherit a dead world. This generation is aware of the great danger facing the world, so it also has the responsibility and ability to take action before it is too late.

Christianity

Just because humans were put in charge of Creation does not give us permission to abuse, spoil, waste, or destroy what God has made. God's glory is shown in the natural world. Christians oppose all thoughtless exploitation of nature that threatens to destroy it and human life as well.

Hinduism

Nature is sacred and the Divine is expressed through all nature's forms. Nature cannot be destroyed without humankind itself being ultimately destroyed. People must rediscover the ancient tradition of reverence for life. It is no longer a question of spiritual merit or sympathy for nature, but one of survival.

Islam

God's oneness (unity) is reflected in people's oneness with creation. Allah has made people stewards of the Earth and he will hold them to account for their actions. This means that Allah's trustees (all Muslims) are responsible for maintaining the unity of his creation, the integrity of the Earth, its plants and animals, its wildlife and its natural environment. Submission to Allah's will should govern all decisions.

Judaism

God placed humans in charge of nature but he expected people to act with justice and compassion towards the natural world. Now the environment is in danger of being poisoned and various species, both plant and animal, are becoming extinct. So Jews must put the defence of nature at the centre of their concerns.

Sikhism

God brought the world into being, sustains, nourishes and protects it. Plant and animal conservation is a religious duty. Humans need to use the Earth to sustain their lives but should not exhaust its resources, pollute it or destroy it.

Objectives

Understand the responses made by religious leaders and believers to environmental issues and sustainable development.

∞ links

For more about the Assisi and Ohito Declarations, and the spiritual principles made at Ohito, see pages 14–15.

A *Christians oppose all thoughtless exploitation of nature*

Activities

1 Explain what religious leaders have done in response to environmental problems.

2 Choose a statement from one religion and explain carefully what you think it means humans should do.

Discussion activity 👤👤👤

With a partner or in a small group, discuss the following statement. Give reasons for your opinions and make sure you think about different points of view. Make notes of your discussion and examples of religious teachings and responses, which you can use when revising.

'Religious leaders are not doing enough to save the planet.'

Religious believers and the environment

The WWF and the British government regard faith groups as vital partners in working towards sustainable development. In a recent joint report they noted that many faith groups are already engaged in international, national and local work around environmental issues. Faith groups promote trade justice (fair trade), and urge people to think carefully about the choices they make as consumers. The report has a comprehensive list of religious organisations and websites that are campaigning for or educating about sustainable development.

In addition to these environmental faith groups, religious charities that work for the poor in the developing world are linking that work to sustainable development. The Catholic Agency for Overseas Development (CAFOD) has a 'Live Simply' campaign and Christian Aid has projects on climate change and fair trade. These are all part of the belief that justice for the poor involves richer nations using less of the world's scarce resources.

Research activity 🔍

Using the internet or a library, find out how a religious charity or religious environmental group is promoting sustainable development. You can find information about fair trade, CAFOD and Christian Aid using the references in the Links. Explain some different ways believers work for the environment. Record your information to use when revising for the examination.

∞ links

To read the report in full and access the list of campaign groups and sites, go to:
www.sd-commission.org.uk

AQA Examiner's tip

You need to be able to apply the beliefs, teachings, sacred texts or statements by contemporary religious leaders to the issues discussed in this chapter.

∞ links

Find out more at:
www.fairtrade.org.uk
www.traidcraftshop.co.uk
www.cafod.org.uk
www.christianaid.org.uk

B *Some of the work done by religious charities, such as CAFOD, Fairtrade and Christian Aid*

Extension activity

1. Drawing on your research and any other information you have, consider the following questions. Make notes on key points that you can use when revising for the examination.

   a. Do you think it is possible to act morally (ethically) in industry and commerce at all times? Explain your opinions.

   b. Do you think people would stop buying cheap clothing if they knew more about how it was damaging the lives of workers and the planet?

   c. Should religious people behave differently in relation to these issues? Refer to religious teachings to support your views.

Summary

You should now be able to explain the statements made by religious leaders about the environment and describe what religious believers are doing to look after the world and to encourage sustainable development and fair trade.

2

Religion and planet Earth – summary

For the examination you should now be able to:

✔ explain religious views about the nature of planet Earth (awe and wonder)

✔ explain religious beliefs about the origins of life and their implications for the care of and responsibility for the planet (stewardship)

✔ describe environmental problems and their implications for the future of the planet, such as:

- the emissions from cars, factories, waste
- pollution (e.g. acid rain, oil spills, toxic chemicals, pesticides)
- destruction of natural habitat and deforestation
- use and abuse of natural resources (e.g. oil)

✔ explain the debate about climate change (global warming) and describe the effects of climate change on the planet, such as severe weather, droughts, floods, famine, destruction of crops, effects on plants and animals

✔ describe the work being done to look after the world, such as conservation, Earth Summits, international action, targets to reduce carbon emissions or greenhouse gases, and sustainable development

✔ explain religious attitudes and responses to these issues, using religious texts, teachings and arguments where appropriate.

Sample answer

1 Write an answer to the following exam question:

'It's no good trying to save the rainforests if this means putting thousands of people out of work.'

Do you agree? Give reasons for your answer, showing that you have thought about more than one point of view. Refer to religious arguments in your answer.

(6 marks)

2 Read the following sample answer.

> I don't agree. I think we have to save the rainforests because many animals' habitats are being lost. Without the trees in the rainforests global warming will increase. This will affect everybody.

> But, the rainforests are in poor countries. Stopping production will harm the lives of many quite poor people. I think rich countries should help by giving people resources to create different jobs or to replace trees where the forest has been cleared.

3 With a partner, discuss the sample answer. Do you think that there are other things that the student could have included in the answer?

4 What mark would you give this answer out of six? What are the reasons for the mark you have given? Look at the mark scheme in the Introduction on page 7 (AO2) to help you make a decision.

AQA Examination-style questions

1   Look at the picture below and answer the following questions.

(a) What is conservation?   *(1 mark)*

(b) Give two reasons why many religious believers are against deforestation.   *(2 marks)*

(c) 'God gave us the Earth to use, not abuse.' What do you think?
     Explain your opinion.   *(3 marks)*

(d) Explain the attitudes of religious people to global warming.
     Refer to religious teaching in your answer.   *(6 marks)*

> **AQA Examiner's tip** Remember that you may refer to one or more than one religion or denomination in your answer.

(e) 'Religious leaders should do more to save the Earth.' Do you agree?
     Give reasons for your answer, showing that you have thought about more than
     one point of view. Refer to religious arguments in your answer.   *(6 marks)*

> **AQA Examiner's tip** Answer the question 'Do you agree?' first and then give your reasons. No marks are given for your opinion but without it you cannot show evaluation skills required by the levels of response.

3.1 What is prejudice?

■ Introduction

Prejudice means to 'pre-judge' someone unfairly before getting to know them. It can make someone think less of people because of their race, religion, gender, age, and so on. Many prejudiced attitudes are based on **stereotyping** certain groups of people. For example, it would be stereotyping to think that all football supporters are violent.

Discrimination means acting on a prejudice. It can involve treating someone unfairly or preventing them from having equal chances in life. For example, it would be discrimination to refuse to give someone a job because of their religion.

Positive discrimination means treating people more favourably because of who or what they are.

For example, it would be positive discrimination to give wheelchair users front-row seats at a cinema. It is usually used to help people who may not have been given equal opportunities in the past, for example, deliberately employing more women or people from minority ethnic groups.

■ Why are some people prejudiced?

Most people are prejudiced about something. When people travel abroad they may be unwilling to try foreign foods because they are not used to them. Upbringing and culture play a part in whether we are willing to try new things. These are some reasons for prejudice:

- If someone does not know a group of people or understand their culture or background, it is easier to stereotype and reject them. Lack of education can lead to the ignorance that breeds prejudice. This in turn leads to fear of others who are different, in case they change the way of life people are used to.

- Fear and uncertainty about the future can encourage **scapegoating**, or blaming certain groups of people for problems in society. This can seem to justify treating them badly. For example, the Nazis persuaded people that the Jews were to blame for Germany's economic problems to justify extreme discrimination against them.

A *Fifty years ago this man may not have been given a job because of prejudice*

∞ links

You will consider religious teachings on prejudice on pages 58–63.

Key terms

Prejudice: thinking badly of someone because of the group he/she belongs to.

Stereotyping: having an over-simplified mental image of people and applying it to everyone in a group.

Discrimination: actions as a result of prejudice.

Positive discrimination: treating people more favourably because they have been discriminated against in the past.

Scapegoating: blaming certain groups for problems in society.

Research activity

Using the internet or a library, find out the original meaning of the term 'scapegoat'. How is this term used today? How might scapegoating be linked to prejudice? Make notes on key points and revise them so that you can use them in the examination.

- Children whose parents are prejudiced may grow up hearing racist or sexist comments and are likely to imitate them. Friends and neighbours may also reinforce prejudice, since most people feel comfortable around others with similar opinions. Outsiders may be regarded with suspicion.

- People may base their views of others on an expectation of what people from a particular race or religion are like. A bad experience can affect people's expectations of others. For example, if an old person was mugged by a teenager, they might then think all teenagers were thieves.

- The media is an important influence that can reinforce stereotypes, but it can also be a means of breaking them down. Some Italians may complain of being continually shown as gangsters in films. Yet some homosexuals may feel they are portrayed positively in programmes that show them as people like everyone else.

- Some people may be prejudiced against others because they themselves have been the victims of prejudice or discrimination. Their prejudice is the way they cope with being a victim.

B   *Children can learn prejudice*

Effects of prejudice

Prejudice causes great harm. People can be made to feel worthless, frightened and vulnerable just for being who they are. Prejudice has caused the deaths of millions of people. During World War II, six million Jews were killed in Nazi Germany. Genocide (killing whole groups of people) has taken place more recently in the former Yugoslavia and Rwanda. The removal of white farmers from Zimbabwe in 2000 is a type of ethnic cleansing (clearing a country of a particular ethnic group) even if it did not result in their deaths.

Activities

1   Explain, using examples, the difference between prejudice and discrimination.

2   Explain some of the reasons why people are prejudiced.

3   Give three examples of positive discrimination. Is positive discrimination fair?

4   Are all stereotypes negative? Give reasons for your opinion, using examples.

C   *Jews were victims of prejudice in Nazi Germany*

Discussion activity

With a partner or in a small group, discuss whether you have ever been a victim of prejudice or discrimination, or whether you know someone who has. Have you ever acted on your own prejudices? Discuss how it made you feel about yourself and the other people involved.

Summary

You should now be able to explain the meanings of prejudice and discrimination and describe their causes, origins and effects.

AQA *Examiner's tip*

You need to be clear about the difference between prejudice and discrimination as you may be asked to explain this in the examination.

3.2 Types of prejudice

Race and colour

A person's race usually refers to the ethnic or religious group they come from, their nationality or sometimes to the colour of their skin. People speak of 'blacks', 'Asians', 'the Jewish race' or 'the German race'. In the past people used to think humans could be separated into distinct races, which passed their physical characteristics down to the next generation. Scientists now agree that there are no biologically distinct human races, and everyone shares most of the same characteristics.

Descriptions of skin colour can also be misleading. 'white' and 'black' may be used to describe people whose skin is pink and brown. There are all sorts of shades of skin colour, yet black- and brown-skinned people are more likely to be victims of prejudice discrimination.

Racism

Racism is the belief that the colour of a person's skin determines their ability. Racists believe that people of some races are inferior to others. Although it is against the law, racist abuse and even physical assaults do occur. Black football players, even at the top level of their sport, have suffered racist chanting, spitting and objects thrown at them from the crowd. Public bodies, such as the police, armed forces and even the Church, have been accused of having deep-seated racism.

Objectives

Explore different types of prejudice including race, colour and gender.

∞ links

For more about the law and discrimination, see pages 64–65.

A *There is only one human race*

Research activity 🔍

Stephen Lawrence

Using the internet or a library, find out more about the circumstances of the murder of Stephen Lawrence. He was a black teenager who was stabbed to death in London in 1993 by a gang of white youths. Nobody was ever convicted of his murder due to police blunders. How did racism play a part in his murder and in the subsequent actions of the police? Make notes on key points that you can use when revising for the examination.

B *Stephen Lawrence was murdered because of his race*

Gender

A person's gender can be determined by what sex they are, male or female, their sexual identity, and the way they see themselves and relate to the world. Society creates certain expectations for the behaviour of each gender, known as sexual stereotypes. People who do not conform, such as men who want to work in a caring profession, can experience prejudice and discrimination.

Sexism

Sexism is a form of gender prejudice. It means treating people unfavourably because of their gender. Like racism, sexism is against the law, but old attitudes that consider men as superior to women still persist. Stereotyped ideas, such as that women should look after the home and family, have helped to deny women equal opportunities in the workplace.

Extension activity

1 Find out the meaning of the term 'institutional racism'. Explain why you think the police, armed forces and the Church have been accused of 'institutional racism'. Draw on the research you did into the Stephen Lawrence case in your answer.

C *Men and women can experience gender prejudice if they challenge gender stereotypes*

Women's rights

In the past women had few rights: they were not allowed to vote, divorce a husband, or inherit property. They almost entirely had to obey their fathers or husbands. After World War I, when women took over 'men's work' while the men were away fighting, their status began to change. However, it is only in the last 50 years or so that it became accepted that married women could work. Despite this progress, many women still earn less money than men and find it difficult to get promoted to senior positions. Some, along with some men, experience unfair interviews and sexual harassment at work.

Religions teach that women and men are created equal by God. However, some religions think they should have different roles. This does not mean they value women less. Staying home to bring up children in their faith is seen as more important than having a career and making money.

Activities

1 Think of some examples of boys and girls that you know, who do not conform to sexual stereotypes.

a Note down what sort of prejudices they experience.

b Why do you think the right to vote was so important to women? Think about how laws can be changed to prevent discrimination before you answer.

Discussion activity

1 Get into three groups. Each group should discuss one of the following statements, and then report back to the class on the views of the group. What prejudices are present in your class? Take notes on all the presentations to build up a bank of examples that you can refer to when revising for the examination.

- 'Anything boys can do, girls can do better.'
- 'There is only one race – the human race.'
- 'Mothers' Day just reinforces women's traditional roles.'

links

For more about the different religions' teachings on prejudice, see pages 58–63.

Extension activity

2 Find current examples of prejudice or discrimination in the news that you can use to support your answers in the examination. Watch out on the news for new examples and add them to your notes so that your answer can be as current as possible.

AQA Examiner's tip

You need to know why and how people are discriminated against because of their race, colour or gender, and be able to use relevant examples to back up your answers in the examination.

Summary

You should now be able to explain why race, colour and gender might cause some people to be prejudiced.

Religious prejudice

People of all religions have been discriminated against throughout the centuries. Discrimination based on religion or belief is now against the law. Since the terrorist attacks in New York (September 11th 2001) and London (July 7th 2005), Muslims have experienced increasing religious prejudice. Yet Islam as a religion does not accept or support terrorism, and the Muslim community rejects these violent acts. However, because some terrorists claim to be acting in the name of Allah, some people think all Muslims support these crimes.

Jews have suffered religious persecution throughout their history. Roman Catholics have faced discrimination in jobs and other rights in Northern Ireland and elsewhere. Religious persecution can quite often be more about people's ethnic group, tribe, colour or culture rather than just their religion. There is also a difference between prejudice against someone's religion and genuine disagreements with people over their beliefs. Not all arguments between religious groups are based on prejudice. For example, Quakers may disagree with other Christians about fighting in wars. This is because they interpret Jesus' teaching to love one's enemies to mean that wars are always wrong.

Ageism

Ageism (prejudice against someone because of their age, leading to discrimination) is often based on stereotypes. For example, some people wrongly think that all young people are rude, irresponsible hooligans and old people are 'past it'. Ageism usually refers to discrimination against older people because employers think they are incapable of doing certain jobs. Younger people have better chances of being hired. Employers may think that their health, energy and productivity may be better than someone nearing retirement. Some employers now realise that older people have a wealth of experience, just as young people have potential. Age discrimination is against the law.

Objectives

Explore different types of prejudice including those based on religion, age, disability, class, lifestyle and looks (or physical appearance).

A The Muslim community demonstrating that it rejects violence

AQA Examiner's tip

Remember that not all arguments between religions show prejudice (judging them before the facts are known). Some religions understand each other well, but genuinely disagree with each other about certain issues or beliefs.

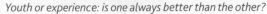

B Youth or experience: is one always better than the other?

Disability discrimination

Most people would consider it wrong to call a disabled person names. However, discrimination can occur against people with a **disability** in the workplace or when they are denied access to services. Sometimes this is unintentional. Disabled access ramps, lifts, toilets and other facilities have only recently become normal in public buildings and firms. People with learning disabilities sometimes experience prejudice because people do not understand their problems.

Prejudice based on class, lifestyle and looks

Social class (people's position in society) was often determined by their family background, education, job and wealth. Today, people move between classes or fall into different ones. For example, bright working-class children may go to university and become middle class. Many celebrities have great wealth, but may not have had much formal education or come from upper-class families. Money is often the biggest influence on a person's **lifestyle**: their interests, activities, opinions, possessions and spending habits. Great attention is paid to a celebrity's looks, their clothes, their body and their fashion sense. People who do not conform to these images can often experience prejudice.

Lifestyle choices influence health. People who smoke, drink alcohol, eat a poor diet and do not exercise are much more likely to have health problems. The government is highlighting obesity as a problem in society. This, along with media images of thin models, encourages others to look down on people with weight problems. Discrimination on these grounds may also occur in the workplace, but it is difficult to prove.

C   *The law requires disabled people to be given equal opportunities and access to public areas*

D   *Celebrity lifestyles shown in the media seem to consist of parties and shopping trips*

Research activity

Using the internet or a library, find some examples of the ways certain groups of people are portrayed in the media. You could look in magazines for pictures of celebrities, or draw on the examples given in this section. Record your findings and revise these in preparation for the examination.

Discussion activity

As a group or in pairs discuss the statement below. Consider both sides of the argument, and note down the key points and revise these when preparing for the examination.

'Old people always think they know best.'

Activities

1   Explain how and why people are discriminated against because of one of these things: religion, age, disability, class, lifestyle or looks.

2   Think of your school or college building. Could disabled students have equal access to a good education there? Give reasons for your answer.

3   Explain the kind of prejudice there might be about a person's looks.

4   Give an example of discrimination against someone because of their lifestyle.

AQA   Examiner's tip

You need to know why and how people are discriminated against because of their religion, age, disability, class, lifestyle and looks (physical appearance) so that you can answer a question about these issues in the examination.

Summary

You should now be able to explain why prejudice occurs based on religion, age, disability, class, lifestyle and looks, and be able to give examples of at least one of these.

3.4 Religious attitudes to prejudice

Tolerance

The Universal Declaration of Human Rights issued in 1948 said that all human beings are born free and equal in dignity and rights. Everyone has the right to think what they want and express their opinions. This is the basis of **tolerance**. Tolerance is accepting all people and valuing their contribution to life and society. People should be allowed to keep their own beliefs, practices and ways of life as long as they do not harm others or break the law.

Tolerance towards other people who are different or hold different beliefs does not mean agreeing with them. It means respecting their rights to hold beliefs that some people may think are wrong, without oppressing or persecuting them. There are limits to tolerance, however. Racist or other prejudiced views harm other people, so cannot be tolerated.

Objectives

Understand the meaning of the concepts of tolerance, justice, harmony and the value of the individual.

Consider how religious attitudes to prejudice and discrimination are based on these concepts.

A *People have different beliefs, but religions teach tolerance*

Justice

All religions teach that people are equal. This means that all people have the same value and worth and equal human rights to live and work freely, and be happy and at peace. This does not mean everyone is the same or has equal advantages in life – they obviously do not. Religious believers think people should be treated with **justice**, that is, fairly and according to the law. If laws are unjust, religious people should work to change them.

Harmony

Harmony means living at peace with others. It requires people to act justly and have tolerance and understanding of others, even when they are different. Many religious believers have a sense of community, feel responsible for each other and share the same values. They believe that practising kindness, compassion and generosity within their religious communities will help them to live in harmony with people in the wider community in which they live.

Key terms

Tolerance: respecting the beliefs and practices of others.

Justice: bringing about what is right, fair, according to the law or making up for what has been done wrong.

Harmony: living in peace with others.

The value of the individual

Human rights are based on the religious belief that each individual is created by God and has a special value to him. Each person is unique and made in God's image. Therefore, humans should treat each other as equals, regardless of race, colour, religion or gender, and all should have the same rights and opportunities.

Case study

The Universal Declaration of Human Rights

Human rights are the basic rights and freedoms that everyone is entitled to. The ideas and values in the Universal Declaration of Human Rights can be traced back through history. The same beliefs and values were present in the world's ancient cultures and religions. From early times laws were made to protect people against abuses of their rights to live freely and try to be happy.

Research activity

A simplified version of the Universal Declaration of Human Rights can be found at the site listed in the Links. Choose three of these human rights you think are the most important and explain why. Note down the facts and your opinions that you could use in the examination.

B Can you identify the human rights depicted in these images?

Activities

1 How would believing in tolerance and justice affect people's attitudes towards prejudice and discrimination?

2 Explain how religious believers try to develop harmony.

Discussion activity

1 In groups, discuss one of the following statements. Try to consider different opinions. Make notes on key points and revise these in preparation for the examination.

a 'Everyone should have the right to free speech, even racists.'

b 'Religious students should be allowed to wear turbans, hijabs and so on in school.'

C

links

A simplified version of the Universal Declaration of Human Rights can be found at:

www.bbc.co.uk/worldservice/people/features/ihavearightto/four_b/all_rights.html

AQA Examiner's tip

'Explain' means interpret, analyse or give reasons for something. This tests your understanding. In Activity 2 you need to give examples of some ways believers try to develop harmony and then explain how those ways develop harmony.

AQA Examiner's tip

You need to be able to explain the key terms on these pages and apply them to the issue of prejudice in your examination.

Summary

You should now be able to explain the concepts of tolerance, justice, harmony and the value of the individual, and show how religious attitudes to prejudice and discrimination are based on these concepts.

3.5 Western faiths

Christianity

All Christians agree that discrimination goes against the idea of God's design. Christians believe that God created men and women in his own image; therefore all are of equal value. Jesus's teaching to 'love your neighbour as yourself' was explained in the parable of the Good Samaritan. In this story, the Samaritan, an enemy of the Jews, was the hero. Jesus taught that anyone who needs help, regardless of background, should be treated kindly. He welcomed tax collectors and sinners to God's kingdom. He healed sick and disabled people, even the servant of a Roman centurion. He treated people of different religious beliefs with respect. St Paul summed up Christian teaching on equality in his letter to the Galatians (see Beliefs and teachings).

Christians today actively fight racial discrimination. In 2005, Anglicans elected their first black archbishop, John Sentamu, although there are still not many black or Asian priests. Some Protestant denominations and Anglicans allow women to be priests or ministers, but the Roman Catholic and Orthodox Churches do not. They do not think this is discrimination, but that women have different roles to play.

Islam

Muslims believe that Allah created all people equal, whatever their race, gender or background. They believe that their differences show the wonderful variety of God's creations. Muhammad preached against slavery and taught that someone's tribe, race, colour or traditions are not an excuse for unjust treatment. Equality in the sight of Allah is shown on hajj, the pilgrimage to Makkah, where all wear simple white garments regardless of racial or social status. The worldwide Muslim community contains people of every background. Islamic law is based on justice and protects the right of non-Muslims living in Muslim countries to practise their religion.

Women are equal to men but have different roles, most importantly to bring up their children in their faith. Most women do not pray with the men at the mosque and a woman cannot become an imam. However, Muhammad taught that a believer who does good work for Allah's sake, whether a man or a woman, will be rewarded.

Judaism

Jews believe that humanity was created by God in his image so all are equal in God's sight. The Torah commands 'love your neighbour as yourself' and says that foreigners, like the poor, should be treated with compassion. The prophets Amos and Isaiah taught that God was more pleased by social justice than religious ceremonies. The prophet Jonah's narrow-minded prejudice against the people of Nineveh city was punished by God. Jews have been victims of anti-Semitism (hatred of Jews), persecution and terrorism, so they recognise how evil racism is. They accept converts from other races and there are many African Jews.

Objectives

Explore religious attitudes towards prejudice and discrimination in Christianity, Islam and Judaism.

Understand how teachings about equality are put into practice.

Beliefs and teachings

'There is neither Jew nor Greek, slave nor free, male nor female, for you are all one in Christ Jesus.'

St Paul, in his letter to the Galatians 3:28

Beliefs and teachings

'Allah does not look upon your outward appearance; He looks upon your hearts and your deeds.'

Hadith

links

For a definition of prejudice and discrimination see pages 52–53 and for more information on religious attitudes to prejudice see pages 58–59.

Beliefs and teachings

'And you are to love those who are aliens, for you yourselves were aliens in Egypt.'

Deuteronomy 10:19

All Jews agree that men and women have equal status, but differ about their roles. Orthodox Jews do not allow women to sit with them in the synagogue, handle the Torah scrolls or become rabbis. Women can have careers as long as they fulfil their important roles as wife and mother, responsible for bringing up children in the faith. Reform Jews allow women to be rabbis, sit with the men and handle the Torah scrolls.

Research activity

Using the internet or a library, find out what religious organisations like Churches Together in Britain and Ireland or the Jewish Council for Racial Equality do to combat prejudice. Record your findings to use as examples in the examination.

A   *The hajj demonstrates equality in the sight of Allah*

Activities

1   Explain the teachings about equality from one religion.

2   From the example of Jesus, what should a Christian attitude be towards disabled people?

3   How do Muslims show their belief in the equality of all races?

4   How could people treat foreigners with compassion today?

5   Some religious believers think women are equal but have different roles. Is this true equality? Explain your opinions.

Discussion activity

With a partner or in a small group, discuss the statement below. Consider different viewpoints, and refer to religious teachings. Make notes on key points and revise these in preparation for the examination.

'Single faith schools encourage prejudice.'

∞links

Find out more at:
www.ctbi.org.uk
www.jcore.org.uk

AQA Examiner's tip

When describing religious attitudes, you can gain higher marks by quoting or referring to the teachings from sacred texts or religious authorities that support them.

Summary

You should now be able to explain religious attitudes towards prejudice and discrimination, the teachings on which they are based, and how Christianity, Islam and Judaism put teachings about equality into practice.

3.6 Eastern faiths

Buddhism

The Buddha left his wealthy lifestyle as he realised that wealth did not bring happiness. He rejected the caste system, which divided people into classes. He thought people only created divisions to feel superior to others.

The Buddha taught that everyone has equal potential for reaching enlightenment. Right Action, Right Speech and loving-kindness, require Buddhists to treat people equally, avoid prejudiced talk and show tolerance and consideration. All members of the sangha (community) are equal. Although reluctant at first, because of social conditions at that time, Buddah ordained women. Buddhists welcome men and women of all races and nationalities. In countries where the culture allows it, women can become nuns. The Dalai Lama, a Buddhist leader, believes that people need to increase mutual understanding and respect, whatever their culture or beliefs. They do not have to agree with each other or go to the same temple to achieve this.

Beliefs and teachings

'If we are full of good will, our own mind, our own heart, is the temple. Kindness, alone, is enough.'

The Dalai Lama

Hinduism

A Hindu's duty is to regard everyone with respect because they have been created by God. God is present in every living being and loves all creatures equally. All men and women of any caste can reach the spiritual goal of moksha (release) if they seek God. Traditionally Hindus were divided into four groups or castes:

- Brahmins (priests and teachers)
- Kshatriyas (soldiers and rulers)
- Vaishyas (merchants and farmers)
- Shudras (labourers and craftsmen).

People could not easily marry someone of a different caste or mix freely with them. Below the Shudras, and not part of the caste system, were the 'untouchables' who had few rights. Discrimination against them was outlawed in 1949, influenced by Mahatma Gandhi's support for them. However, since a person's caste is believed to be the result of bad karma from a previous life, prejudice against lower castes and untouchables still exists. Hinduism has many paths to God so Hindus are tolerant of other people's religions.

Men and women are equal, but have different roles. Priests must be men and it is generally men who perform religious ceremonies. Women perform puja (prayer) in the home. Women now have more rights to be educated, take up well-paid jobs and own property. In 1966 Indira Gandhi was made the first female prime minister of India.

Beliefs and teachings

'The things which divide and separate people – race, religion, gender, social position ... are all illusory.'

Dhammapada 6

A Buddhists welcome men and women of all races and nationalities

B Hindu women now have the right to a career

Sikhism

Sikhs believe that all men and women are equal; they are all children of God, their creator. Since God has no colour or form, it is wrong to discriminate on grounds of race, gender or religion. Sikhs are tolerant of all religions and the Guru Granth Sahib contains Muslim and Hindu writings.

Guru Nanak thought the idea that someone was 'untouchable' was mere superstition. He banned the custom of a wife throwing herself on her husband's funeral pyre. Women deserve respect as it is through them that the human race continues.

In the gurdwara everyone sits on the floor to show they are equal. Men and women usually sit separately, but women take a full part in worship. Any educated Sikh can be a granthi, the person who reads the Guru Granth Sahib or leads the service. Non-Sikhs are made welcome, offered karah parshad (blessed food) and invited to eat at the langar (kitchen). Vegetarian food is provided so no one feels excluded. Sikhism is open to people of all races. Women can become Khalsa Sikhs and granthis. They can marry members of other faiths as long as they can remain Sikhs.

C *Sikh women generally worship separately from men*

Beliefs and teachings

'Know people by the light which illuminates them, not by their caste.'

Guru Granth Sahib 349

Research activity

Using what you have learned in these sections, and the internet or a library, find out more about the role women play in one religion. Are they treated as equals? Make notes on key points and revise these in preparation for the examination.

Discussion activity

1 Choose one of the statements below and discuss it in pairs. Get together with another pair and share your opinions and ideas, referring to religious teachings. Then create a set of notes on key points and revise these in preparation for the examination.

a 'The belief that women are equal but different leads to discrimination against them.'

b 'People are prejudiced against anyone who is religious.'

Activities

1 Explain the teachings about equality from Buddhism, Hinduism or Sikhism.

2 What is the caste system? Who is an 'untouchable'?

3 Why did both Guru Nanak and the Buddha reject the caste system?

4 Explain how Sikhs show their belief in equality in their worship.

Summary

You should now be able to explain religious attitudes towards prejudice and discrimination, the teachings on which they are based, and how Buddhism, Hinduism and Sikhism put teachings about equality into practice.

AQA *Examiner's tip*

When describing religious attitudes, you will gain marks by quoting or referring to the teachings from sacred texts or religious authorities that support them.

Response to prejudices

■ Society and the law

Democracy and human rights are founded on religious principles of equality and justice for all. These ideas are central to the laws created to combat prejudice and discrimination. The UK government is a secular government, but religious people would support any laws that promote and secure principles and beliefs that are shared with religions. In Muslim countries Shari'ah law is based on religious principles.

Britain has passed a number of laws against discrimination:

- Sex Discrimination Act 1975
- Race Relations Act 1976
- Disability Discrimination Act 1995
- Equality Act 2006 (against religious discrimination and ageism).

These laws mean that all people should have equal rights at work and equal pay for the same type of work. They should have equal chances to get a good education or healthcare, go to a restaurant or the cinema, buy things and do whatever they want within the law. If someone thinks they are being discriminated against they can take the person to court. Prejudice is harder to stop than discrimination, because you cannot arrest people for their attitudes, only for their actions. Schools and the media have an important part to play in getting the message across that people should be treated equally.

■ Individuals

Case study

Anthony Walker

Sixth former Anthony Walker was killed with an ice axe in Merseyside in 2005. His killers, Paul Taylor, 20, and Michael Barton, 17, had killed him simply for being black, even though Taylor had been to primary school with him. Anthony's mother, Gee, said she felt no hate for her son's killers, only pity for their families. As a Christian, she had brought her children up to stand for peace, love and forgiveness. The pain at losing a child has no comparison, but Gee believed that she would be dishonouring her son's memory if she did not forgive his killers. She says that parents and teachers must instil respect, tolerance and kindness in young people. They should not feel ashamed of their race. They should only be ashamed of themselves if they do nothing to promote unity. Her family has set up a charity in Anthony's name to fight racism.

A *Gee Walker, the mother of the late Anthony Walker*

■ Groups

The Corrymeela Community

The Corrymeela Community was founded by Catholics and Protestants in Northern Ireland during a time when violence between them was tearing their country apart. It is a Christian community that promotes peace, tolerance and respect by providing a place where people from different religions can meet and talk freely.

Every year, more than 8,000 people explore ways of moving away from violence and finding more constructive ways of working together. The success of Corrymeela has affected even those politicians who had not been able to agree. The politicians accepted Corrymeela's guiding principle that building relationships of trust is the only way real peace and reconciliation can come about. Since the Good Friday Agreement, the community continues its work of breaking down religious barriers.

B 'The Troubles' – Corrymeela was set up to help people to move away from violence

Activities

1   Explain how UK society has responded to injustices like prejudice and discrimination.

2   Explain how the Corrymeela Community combats prejudice and discrimination. How does its work reflect Christian teachings on this issue?

Discussion activities

1   Discuss this statement as a class.

'Tolerance and harmony are impossible in society today.'

2   With a partner or in a small group, discuss the case of Anthony Walker. What do you think of Gee Walker's attitude to her son's killers? Give reasons for your opinions and include reference to her religious beliefs.

3   Review your class discussion, drawing on what you have said about Gee Walker. Do her attitude and actions make you more hopeful for tolerance and harmony in society? Make notes on all steps of this activity and revise these in preparation for the examination.

AQA Examiner's tip

Remember that secular society's response to prejudice through laws is based on what were originally religious beliefs that all people were created equal by God with certain human rights.

Extension activity

Using the internet (see the Links) or a library, find out more about the various laws listed at the start of this section. Find out three ways in which each law supports equality. Record your findings and revise these so that you can use them as examples in your examination.

∞ links

Find out more at:

www.direct.gov.uk (search for 'Introduction to discrimination', click on the link and research different types of discrimination)

Summary

You should now be able to describe responses to prejudice and discrimination by society, the law, individuals and groups and explain how religious beliefs influence those responses.

3.8 Mahatma Gandhi

Mahatma Gandhi

Mahatma Gandhi was a Hindu born in India in 1869. Originally called Mohandas, he has been given the title 'Mahatma' (great soul), which is now sometimes used as his first name. He trained as a lawyer in England, and at the age of 24, he went to South Africa to work in an Indian law firm. Whilst there, he personally experienced racial prejudice and discrimination under the apartheid laws. These laws kept blacks, other non-white groups known as coloureds and whites separated in all areas of life, and discriminated heavily against non-whites.

Objectives

Understand how Mahatma Gandhi fought against prejudice and discrimination.

AQA Examiner's tip

'Describe' means give a detailed account of the facts. You do not need to explain them. This tests knowledge.

Research activity

Using the internet or a library, research someone who has campaigned against prejudice and discrimination for the religion(s) that you are studying.

A Ghandi showed his love for the poor by dressing like them

Gandhi's South African campaigns

As a Hindu, Gandhi practised non-violence and believed in the presence of truth in each person's soul. He believed that the only way of treating others is to love them. He thought that the best way to fight prejudice was peacefully, refusing to cooperate with the authorities who discriminated against people. He started to campaign for the rights of Indians living in South Africa. He used a method of non-violent mass civil disobedience. In other words, thousands of people merely refused to register for an unfair poll tax. Although many were beaten, jailed and even shot, eventually after seven years the poll tax was dropped. He also succeeded in making Indian marriages legal in South Africa.

links

For more about apartheid, see pages 70–71.

Gandhi's Indian campaigns

Gandhi returned to India in 1915 and used his peaceful methods to fight against the British who ruled India. He also campaigned to help the poorest people, who, under the caste system, were not allowed to associate with others, even while worshipping, because they were considered unclean. Gandhi called them Harijans (children of God) and led them by the hand into the temples that had excluded them. He brought women and people of all castes into the Indian National Congress. After a massacre of unarmed civilians by British troops in Amritsar in 1919, Gandhi led a nationwide campaign of not cooperating with British rule. This included boycotting British goods and refusing to pay taxes, particularly the tax on salt. He led thousands in a march to the sea where they made salt by evaporating sea water. Although he was arrested and imprisoned for two years, the campaign succeeded and the tax was stopped.

Gandhi's final years and legacy

Gandhi began to wear a dhoti (loincloth) like the poor, to show his belief in equality and peace. He would sometimes fast to purify himself spiritually and identify with the poor, but also to protest. His actions eventually resulted in better treatment for the poor, particularly when the British gave India independence. This came about partly as a result of Gandhi's influence. He then tried to make peace between Hindus and Muslims over the role of Pakistan, before he was assassinated in 1948 by a Hindu extremist. Three million people took part in his funeral procession. Today his life is commemorated by a national holiday on the 2nd of October in India. Gandhi continues to inspire people to take action against injustice today.

Activities

1. Describe the prejudice Gandhi found in South Africa and India and explain what he did about it.

2. Why do you think he was given the title 'Mahatma'?

3. Explain the religious beliefs that influenced his actions.

B *Gandhi continues to be in the thoughts of the Indian people*

⃝⃝ links

For an explanation of the caste system, see page 62.

Discussion activity

In small groups, discuss this statement:

'If people want to change the world, they should start by changing themselves.'

Do you agree? Try to think of other points of view as well. You may wish to refer to an example such as Gandhi. Make a note of the key points of your discussion and revise these so that you can use them in the examination.

AQA Examiner's tip

You should be able to use Mahatma Gandhi as an example of how a Hindu has challenged prejudice and discrimination by following Hindu beliefs and teachings.

Summary

You should now be able to explain how Mahatma Gandhi challenged prejudice and discrimination in South Africa and India.

3.9 Martin Luther King

Martin Luther King

The Reverend Dr Martin Luther King, Jr. was born in Atlanta, Georgia, USA in 1929. When he was 18, he became a Christian minister, like his father.

Segregation and discrimination

In America at that time, black people faced awful prejudice and discrimination. Segregation (a policy of separating blacks and whites) meant that black children had to attend different schools from white children. Often these schools had poorer facilities, books and equipment than the 'white-only' schools. Black people could not use the same swimming pools or sit in the same restaurants as white people. They earned half as much as white people and many were not allowed to vote. A racist group, the Ku Klux Klan, used violence against black people or anyone who sympathised with them.

These injustices went against Martin Luther King's Christian beliefs. He wanted black people to be treated fairly, so he set out to change the laws by persuading people through argument. Inspired by the life of Jesus and the ideas of the Hindu leader, Mahatma Gandhi, he was determined to fight racism without using violence.

The civil rights movement

In 1955, in Montgomery, Alabama, a woman called Rosa Parks was arrested for refusing to give up her seat on a bus to a white man. The law said black people had to sit at the back of the bus. If it was crowded and a white person got on, they had to give up their seat for the white person. Martin Luther King organised a 'bus boycott'. Thousands of black people refused to travel on the buses until the law was changed over a year later. During this time, King was arrested, his home was bombed and he received death threats to himself and his family.

The boycott's success and King's personal courage earned him great respect. He became leader of the 'civil rights movement', which organised campaigns for black voter registration, better education and housing for black people, and desegregation of public facilities. He and other black people sat down in restaurants that refused to serve them and waited to be arrested. The television pictures of people, including children, being attacked by police dogs did a great deal to persuade all Americans that the laws were unjust.

Objectives

Understand how Martin Luther King challenged discrimination and prejudice.

⬭ links

For more about Mahatma Gandhi, see pages 66–67. Segregation is similar to apartheid, which is covered on pages 70–71.

A *Martin Luther King, delivering his historic 'I have a dream' speech*

King led hundreds of thousands of people in protest marches and inspired people with his words. At the historic march on Washington DC in 1963, he delivered a famous speech in which he said that he had a dream that one day people would judge his children on what kind of people they were rather than on the colour of their skin. He spoke of his hope that people of all races and religions would join hands and thank God that they were free at last.

King's final years and legacy

In 1964, King was awarded the Nobel Peace Prize. The following year the US Supreme Court gave equal voting rights to black people though America was not to elect a black president until 40 years after King's death. Martin Luther King was assassinated in 1968 at the age of 39. Americans remember his great contribution to the fight against prejudice every January on Martin Luther King Day.

B   In 2008, America elected a black president, Barack Obama

Research activity

1   Using the Internet or a library, look up the famous 'I have a dream' speech of Martin Luther King. The following website will help you. www.usconstitution.net/dream.html

Discussion activity

Discuss the following statement in small groups. Consider everything you have learned so far about racism. Be sure to consider all points of view, including religious arguments or beliefs. Record your discussion and revise it in preparation for the examination.

'Racist laws can be changed, but prejudice still exists.'

Research activity

2   Using the internet or a library, find out more about the black leader Malcolm X. He was a Muslim who did not agree with non-violence as a means to achieve equality. Should violence be used to fight racism? Explain your opinion, making a record of key points out about Malcolm X and revise these so that you can use them in the examination.

AQA Examiner's tip

'Explain' means analyse, interpret or give reasons for something. In Activity 3 you need to interpret what King said was his dream. Remember, always read or look at the stimulus in the examination.

Summary

You should now be able to explain how Martin Luther King challenged racist laws in the United States of America.

Activities

1   Describe examples of prejudice and discrimination in southern USA at the time of the civil rights movement.

2   Describe three things Martin Luther King did to challenge prejudice and discrimination. How do you think his Christian beliefs influenced his actions?

3   Explain the meaning of Martin Luther King's 'dream'. Try to relate his views to Christian teachings on the subject of prejudice.

Desmond Tutu

Desmond Tutu was born in Klerksdorp, South Africa in 1931. He became an Anglican priest in 1960 at a time when the apartheid system denied many black and 'coloured' people their rights.

Apartheid

Apartheid means 'separateness'. It was a South African policy that kept black and white people apart. Black people were not allowed to vote, even though they were in the majority. They did not have equal access to jobs, housing, education or other public services. White people were not allowed to marry non-white people. These injustices were reinforced by the Dutch Reformed Church, who taught that God had created white people superior to other races. They thought the racist apartheid laws were God's will. Other Christians disagreed and accused them of misusing the Bible just to keep white people in power. Many years later, the Dutch Reformed Church accepted that their racist views were anti-Christian and made a public apology.

Anti-apartheid campaigns

Desmond Tutu became the first black general secretary of the South African Council of Churches in 1978. He used his position to campaign for equal civil rights for all and a common system of education for all children. He worked to get rid of South Africa's unfair 'pass laws', which limited employment prospects and travel for black people. People were separated based on race and forced to live in certain areas called 'homelands'. These were poorer, rural areas where there was not much work. Many black people were arrested if caught outside the homelands without their pass.

Non-violent protest

Desmond Tutu supported non-violent protests, like Martin Luther King and Mahatma Gandhi. In the black township of Soweto young people had protested a ruling that said they had to do half their lessons in Afrikaans (the language of the racist government). The police opened fire on them and around 600 young people were killed. Desmond Tutu led a peaceful march through Soweto to protest the actions of the police. He saved the life of a black policeman by throwing himself over him when a crowd tried to stone the man to death. He organised petitions and called for other countries to support economic sanctions (penalties) against South Africa. In this way, pressure was put on the South African government to change the apartheid laws. He was an outspoken critic of the racist laws in his preaching and writing. He was awarded the Nobel Peace Prize in 1984 for his leadership and for 'the courage and heroism shown by black South Africans in their use of peaceful methods in the struggle against apartheid'.

Objectives

Understand Desmond Tutu's work against prejudice and discrimination.

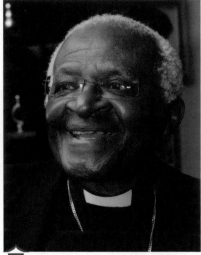

A Desmond Tutu

∞ links

For more about Mahatma Gandhi and Martin Luther King see pages 66–69.

Research activity 🔍

Use a library or the internet to extend your knowledge and understanding of apartheid and Desmond Tutu's work in fighting it. You can use what you find out as an example in the examination.

After apartheid

In 1986 Tutu became the first black Archbishop of Cape Town, the leader of the Anglican Church in South Africa. When South Africa became a multiracial republic in 1994, Archbishop Tutu led the Truth and Reconciliation Commission. This looked into human rights abuses during apartheid and protected people from being taken to court if they were willing to confess the wrongs they had done. As a Christian, Tutu believed in the importance of admitting wrongdoing and asking for forgiveness from God and from others. His report strongly criticised both sides, each of whom had committed violent crimes. He spoke about the new South Africa as the 'rainbow people of God'. Archbishop Tutu believes that being a Christian involves working for justice and equality.

> 66 *True Christian worship includes the love of God and the love of neighbour. The two must go together or your Christianity is false. St John asks, in his First Epistle, how you can say you love God whom you have not seen if you hate your brother whom you have. Our love for God is tested and proved by our love for our neighbour.* 99
>
> *Desmond Tutu in* Hope and Suffering

Activities

1 Explain four ways in which Desmond Tutu worked to overcome prejudice.

2 Why do you think Desmond Tutu chose not to use violent methods to challenge racism? Explain your opinion, referring to religious teachings that may have influenced his thinking.

AQA Examiner's tip

Always give your opinion first in evaluation questions. Then show that you understand why others might disagree with you. Then include religious arguments for the opinions you have expressed.

B *Under apartheid, blacks were not allowed to use the same public services as whites*

Discussion activity

Discuss the following statement in groups. Do you agree or disagree with the statement? Give reasons for your answer, showing that you have thought about more than one point of view. Be sure to include religious arguments in your reasoning, and record the key points made by your group and revise these in preparation for the examination.

'It is impossible to forgive racism.'

Summary

You should now be able to explain how Archbishop Desmond Tutu challenged the system of apartheid in South Africa and the religious beliefs on which his work was based.

3

Religion and prejudice – summary

For the examination you should now be able to:

✔ explain the causes and origins of prejudice, including ignorance, stereotyping, scapegoating, the influence of parents or the media, being a victim of prejudice and personal experience

✔ describe and explain different types of prejudice, including religion, race, colour, gender, age, disability, class, lifestyle and looks

✔ explain the concepts of tolerance, justice, harmony and the value of the individual and apply them to issues of prejudice and discrimination

✔ explain religious attitudes to prejudice and discrimination

✔ describe the effects of prejudice and discrimination, including the idea of positive discrimination

✔ explain religious responses to prejudice and discrimination by individuals, groups, society and the law

✔ describe how religious believers have fought against prejudice, for example, Mahatma Gandhi, Martin Luther King, Desmond Tutu

✔ evaluate religious attitudes and responses to these issues, using religious texts, teachings and arguments where appropriate.

AQA Examiner's tip Remember that you may refer to one or more than one religion or denomination in your answers.

Sample answer

 1 Write an answer to the following examination question:

'You cannot be religious and be prejudiced.'

Do you agree? Give reasons for your answer, showing that you have thought about more than one point of view. Refer to religious arguments in your answer.

(6 marks)

2 Read the following sample answer.

I am not sure about this. Some religious people seem prejudiced against people from different religions. Muslim and Jewish women are not expected to marry outside their faith. In the past some religious groups like the Dutch Reformed Church in South Africa said apartheid was all right and many churches in the southern USA were segregated. However, a Muslim teaching is 'Allah does not look upon your outward appearance, he looks upon your hearts and your deeds'. Muslims regard everyone as equal because it is what kind of person you are, not what you look like, that matters.

3 With a partner, discuss the sample answer. Do you think that there are other things that the student could have included in the answer? What mark would you give this answer out of six?

4 What are the reasons for the mark you have given? Look at the mark scheme in the Introduction on page 7 (AO2) to help you make a decision.

AQA Examination-style questions

1   Look at the statements below and answer the following questions.

> 66 *Prejudice is unfairly judging someone without knowing them.* 99

> 66 *Prejudice can lead to discrimination.* 99

(a) What is stereotyping?   *(1 mark)*

(b) Give two reasons why many religious believers are against discrimination.   *(2 marks)*

(c) 'Religions discriminate against women.' What do you think? Explain your opinion.   *(3 marks)*

(d) Explain the attitudes of religious believers to racism. Refer to religious teaching in your answer.   *(6 marks)*

> **AQA Examiner's tip** Question (d) asks you to explain religious attitudes with reference to religious teaching. Include teachings from holy books or religious leaders that support believers' attitudes towards racism; without this you cannot reach the higher levels.

(e) 'Religious believers have not done enough to fight racism.' Do you agree? Give reasons for your answer, showing that you have thought about more than one point of view. Refer to religious arguments in your answer.   *(6 marks)*

> **AQA Examiner's tip** When asked if you agree with a statement, explain what you think, and why others might disagree. One-sided answers can only achieve four marks. Include religious arguments; without this, you can achieve only three marks.

JOHN KELLY GIRLS
TECHNOLOGY COLLEGE
CREST ROAD NW2 7SN

4.1 The miracle of life

The miracle of life

Most people consider it amazing that a tiny sperm can join with an egg and provide all the information needed to develop into a unique human being. The creation and arrival of a new baby is so special that many parents will say it was one of the best moments of their lives. It is an exciting time for new parents and their joy is shared by grandparents, relatives and friends.

Many people take fertility for granted. However, for a new baby to be conceived there are a lot of factors that have to be just right. One quarter of couples have difficulty starting a family, so fertility is not totally under our control. When a couple who have been trying to have children finally conceive, they truly consider it a **miracle of life**. It is a miracle that helps the human race to continue.

Children as a blessing and gift

Religions often mark the birth of a new baby with a ceremony to show how thankful people are for the gift of new life. Religious people do not see children as a 'right' or something they deserve. Rather they see them as a **blessing**, something wonderful that is given to them by a loving God. Because Buddhists do not believe in God, they do not see children as a gift, but still regard all human beings as precious.

Objectives

Introduce religious ideas about the miracle of life, children being seen as a blessing and a gift, and the sanctity of life in relation to its preservation.

Key terms

Miracle of life: the idea that life is wonderful, amazing or special.

Blessing: the idea that God has favoured a couple with a child.

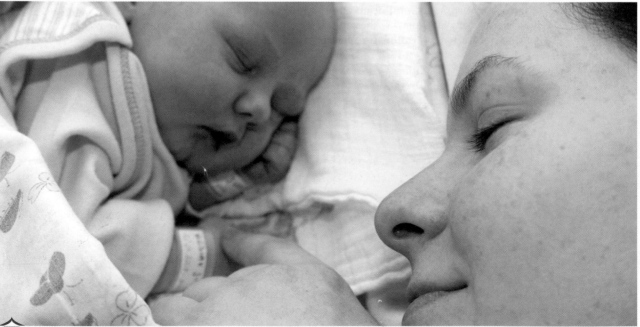

A *The arrival of a new baby: the miracle of life*

Sanctity of life

All religions teach that life is special and precious. This idea is known as the **sanctity of life**. Christians, Jews and Muslims believe that life is sacred or holy because it comes from God. God created life and gave us the natural means to reproduce. As life is God-given and precious, it should be valued and cherished, not destroyed. God gave life, and only God has the right to take life away.

Buddhists, Hindus and Sikhs believe life should be valued as every person deserves a chance to do good and build up good karma. Karma affects what happens to a person either in this life or in a future one. Respecting life creates good karma, but destroying it creates bad karma. Hindus believe in non-violence and Buddhists follow the precept to refrain from taking life. They consider that life is sacred and should be preserved.

Key terms

Sanctity of life: life is sacred because it is God-given.

B   *Life is special and precious*

The miracle of life

Case study

Tibetan Buddhists show their belief in the value of human life by using this comparison. A blind turtle is swimming in a large ocean and comes to the surface once every hundred years. Being reborn as a human is as likely as that turtle putting its head through a small golden ring that is floating on the surface of the water.

Research activity

Using the internet or a library, or by looking at pages 118–119 in this book, find out how one religion celebrates the birth of a baby. What does the celebration show about their beliefs about children?

C   *Baptism: a Christian ritual for a new baby*

Activities

1   Explain why people call the creation of a baby a 'miracle'.

2   Explain the meaning of the term 'sanctity of life'.

3   How might belief in the sanctity of life affect someone's decision about abortion?

4   Read the case study and explain how it shows Buddhist beliefs about human life.

Discussion activity

In pairs discuss the following statement. Try to see different points of view, refer to religious views, and make notes to use in your preparation for the examination.

'People today take the creation of life for granted.'

Summary

You should now be able to explain why religious people see conception and birth as a 'miracle of life' and children as a blessing and gift from God, and the meaning of the sanctity of life in relation to its preservation.

AQA   Examiner's tip

You do not have to be religious to think a newborn baby is a 'miracle of life'. The word 'miracle' here means something amazing and wonderful, not something that goes against the laws of nature.

4.2 When does life begin?

Why it matters

Asking the question, 'When does life begin?' is important, because once a person is alive they have human rights. These include the right to life, which means that killing them is unlawful.

The answer depends on what is meant by 'life'. If life means independent existence outside the mother, it begins at birth, when the child has drawn its first breath and the umbilical cord is severed. However, babies and young children are still dependent on others for survival; they would not live long on their own.

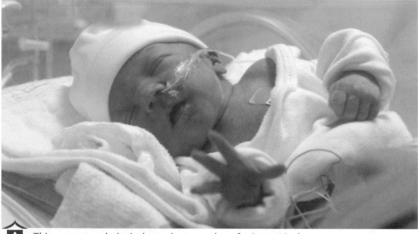

A *This premature baby is dependent on others for its survival*

There are several other views on when a foetus becomes a separate person:

- At **conception**, at the moment when the sperm unites with the ovum (egg). This is when the new being's DNA is fixed, with all the information needed to make a unique individual.
- At the development of the backbone or spinal column, which houses the nervous system. This happens in about the third week of pregnancy.
- When the heart starts beating in about the fourth week of pregnancy.
- When the foetus is **viable**, meaning it could survive outside the womb if born prematurely. It is rare for babies weighing under 500g or who are less than 22 weeks old to survive.

When does life begin?

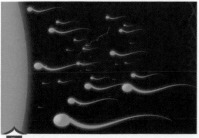

At conception?

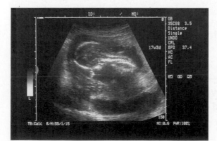

Development of the spine?

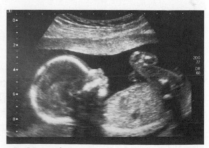

Or 22 weeks?

B

▉ Religious views

Buddhists believe that life begins even before conception because all living things are caught up in the cycle of life, death and rebirth. Therefore, there is no point in time when life 'begins'.

Hindus and Sikhs believe life begins at conception, when something unique comes into being. So do some Jews and some Christians, particularly Roman Catholics. They speak of the embryo (a foetus before eight weeks) as a person, or a potential person, that therefore has rights.

Others, including many Jews, believe the foetus is becoming a person, but is not legally a person until it is born. A Jewish teaching is that the soul becomes present in a person when they leave their mother's womb.

Muslims believe that there is potential life from the moment of conception, but a foetus receives a soul after 120 days. This is therefore when human life really starts.

Activities

1   Explain why some people think life begins at conception.

2   Consider the various opinions about when life begins and explain your own view, giving reasons. Refer to the teachings of at least one religion in your answer.

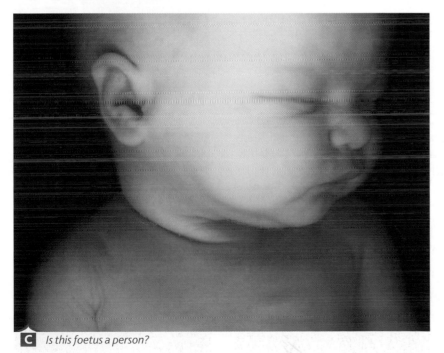

C   *Is this foetus a person?*

Summary

You should now be able to explain the different beliefs about when life begins and why they are important.

⃝⃝ links

You will find more religious teachings and attitudes to these issues on pages 86–91.

Discussion activity

1   In pairs, discuss the following statements. Try to cover different points of view, including religious views. Make notes at the end to refer to when preparing for the examination.

a   'It is nonsense to speak of a moment when life begins.'

b   'A foetus is not a person.'

AQA *Examiner's tip*

Remember that religious people do not always agree about these issues, even within the same religion. In your examination it is useful to say 'some Muslims think…' or 'many Sikhs believe…' to show that you are aware of differences of opinion.

4.3 Quality of life

Quality of life

Quality of life refers to the kind of life the baby will have. It can mean both the physical and mental wellbeing of the child and also the family circumstances into which it is born. Will it live a life without pain and suffering? Will it be able to fulfil its potential? Will it be wanted and loved? It can also refer to the mother's quality of life, and whether the family can support a new baby. For some parents, in some circumstances, the prospect of having a new baby does not fill them with joy. Below are some possible reasons for this.

Severe disability

Babies born with severe mental or physical disabilities may live a life of suffering and pain. They may not be able to enjoy a full life or communicate with others. They may need full-time care, placing extra responsibility on the family.

An unwanted child

Just because a pregnancy is unplanned does not mean that the child is unwanted. Unplanned children are often loved when they arrive. However, in some cases an unplanned pregnancy may cause resentment in a woman whose circumstances are not suitable for motherhood. She may not be able to give the baby the love and care it deserves. If the mother is very young, she may not be ready for such a commitment. The baby's father may not wish to be involved. Occasionally a baby may be conceived through rape.

Poverty

Some people cannot afford a child, particularly if their family is already large, or if they are on a low income. The things needed for a baby are expensive and the quality of life of the whole family may be affected. Parents may be out of work, or if the mother is single, she may have to give up her job to look after a child. Even a child born into a family that is financially well-off may suffer from neglect because its parents may not have time for it, or are unable to provide emotional support.

What justifies ending a pregnancy?

Some parents feel unable to cope with the responsibility of a child in some of these circumstances. However, the issues are complex and need careful consideration.

The child's disability

How severe would a disability have to be, to be a serious threat to quality of life? Many disabled people live happy and productive lives. Disabled UK athletes brought home 102 medals from the Beijing Paralympics. If a child was going to be born deaf or with a cleft palate, would that be enough to justify ending a pregnancy?

A Young motherhood can be very stressful

B Many disabled people can have a good quality of life

Objectives

Explore the concept of quality of life including issues surrounding severe handicaps, unwanted children, poverty and suffering.

Understand how the idea of quality of life is used in arguments about the preservation of life.

Key terms

Quality of life: a measure of fulfilment.

Quality of life

An unplanned pregnancy might be inconvenient, but how badly does the quality of life of the parents have to be affected? Would a holiday or career plans be sufficient reason? Can the child's quality of life in these or similar circumstances be predicted?

Poverty is a relative term. In the developing world, where extreme poverty could be described as a poor quality of life, people often welcome new members of the family. In Britain, the state supports those who are poor. How poor would a person have to be to justify ending a pregnancy?

∞ links

For the legal position on abortion, see page 80. For more on rights and choices, pages 82–85. For religious views see pages 86–91.

Eleanor Simmonds

At 13, Eleanor Simmonds became Britain's youngest individual paralympic gold medal winner at the Beijing Paralympics in 2008. She was born with achondrophasia (dwarfism), but began swimming at the age of five and was inspired to compete when she watched the Athens Paralympics on the television. Her parents moved house to be near the high-performance swimming centre in Swansea where she trains six days a week. She won a gold medal in the 100m freestyle, and then a second gold in the 400m freestyle setting a new world record time of 5 minutes, 41.34 seconds.

C *Eleanor Simmonds*

Case study

Activities

1 Explain the meaning of the term 'quality of life'.

2 Describe in detail two other circumstances, besides those described in this section, when a baby might be unwanted.

3 Read the case study. Who should decide whether someone who has a physical disability will have a good quality of life?

4 Children born into well-off families may also suffer from neglect. Would abortion be justified in this case?

D *Should poverty be a reason for abortion?*

Discussion activity

1 In pairs or groups, discuss one or both of the following statements. Try to consider all points of view, making notes of key points and your own opinion which you can refer to when you are revising in case you are asked about this issue in the examination.

a 'Poor people should not have children because their quality of life will be poor.'

b 'People who do not want children should not get pregnant.

Summary

You should now be able to explain the term 'quality of life' in relation to people with severe disabilities, unwanted children, and those living in poverty and suffering, and discuss how it is used in arguments about the preservation of life.

AQA Examiner's tip

The 'sanctity of life' is often contrasted with the 'quality of life'. Make sure you understand both terms clearly, as you may be asked about this in the examination.

4.4 Abortion and the law

What is abortion?

Abortion is the removal of a foetus from the womb to end a pregnancy. In medical terms, a miscarriage is a form of abortion, but it happens naturally and often without the mother knowing. It is the **deliberate** removal of a foetus from the womb that is the subject of this chapter.

The legal position

Before 1967, abortion was illegal in the whole of the UK. Women wishing to end a pregnancy had to turn to unqualified people who were willing to break the law, sometimes with tragic results.

In England, Scotland and Wales, under the 1967 Abortion Act and the 1990 Human Fertilisation and Embryology Act, abortion is permitted if two doctors agree that one of the following conditions applies:

- The woman might die unless the pregnancy is ended.
- There is a substantial risk of the baby being born severely physically or mentally disabled.
- There is a risk to the woman's physical or mental health.
- There is a risk to the physical or mental health of her existing children.

The 1967 Act allowed abortions up to 28 weeks into a pregnancy. However, with new medical techniques very premature babies can be kept alive. The 1990 Act therefore changed the time limit to 24 weeks. Some people think the time limit should be reduced even further, to as low as 12 weeks. There is no time limit if the mother's life is in danger, if the baby is severely abnormal or if there is grave risk of mental or physical injury to the woman. In an emergency, a second doctor's opinion is not needed.

Abortion is still illegal in Northern Ireland except when a doctor acts to save the life of a mother.

Objectives

Understand what abortion is.

Understand the legal position on abortion, including the 1967 Abortion Act and the 1990 Human Fertilisation and Embryology Act.

links

See pages 86–91 for religious views on abortion.

Key terms

Abortion: the deliberate termination (ending) of a pregnancy, usually before the foetus is 24 weeks and viable.

Activities

1. Explain why you think time limits were put on having an abortion.

2. Why might a woman want an abortion after 24 weeks?

3. Why do you think that the law requires two doctors to agree about an abortion?

4. How might the physical health or mental health of a woman's existing children be damaged if she had a new baby?

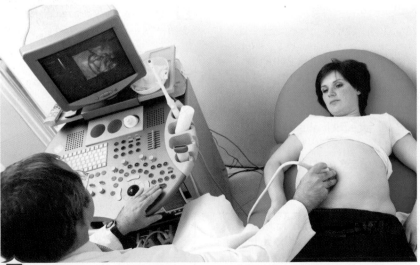

A Early scans mean doctors can now detect problems that might seem to justify an abortion

■ Some other considerations

- Most abortions are carried out early on the grounds of risk to the mother's mental health.

- Some abortions are carried out to reduce the number of foetuses in multiple births where the woman has received fertility treatment. This is to reduce risk to the healthy development of the remaining babies.

- The law does not consider the rights of the father, only those of the foetus, the mother and her existing children.

- Doctors and nurses who disagree with abortion do not have to help carry them out.

- Each year around 185,000 abortions take place.

- Fewer than 200 a year take place after 24 weeks.

Marina

Case study

Marina is 17, eight weeks pregnant and seeking an abortion. The doctor has to decide about her case.

She went out with a man a few times and they agreed to go on holiday to the same place. They had a great time when they were away, but when they came home she saw him once or twice and the relationship faded. He does not know about her pregnancy, nor would he suspect anything as he was using condoms. Marina lives in a small flat and the landlady had made it clear that no children were permitted. She would almost certainly have to quit her job and she has little contact with her parents. She is feeling quite depressed about her situation.

Activity

5 Read the case study. Does Marina's situation merit an abortion according to the law? Explain your opinions.

Discussion activity

1 In pairs or groups, discuss the following statements. Try to include different points of view and to come to an opinion at the end. Make notes that you could refer to in a question on abortion. You may wish to review your discussion after working through the religious views in topics 4.7 to 4.9. Do the religions raise any issues you had not considered?

a 'It is too easy to get an abortion.'

b 'A doctor's job is to save life, not to end it.'

Summary

You should now be able to explain what an abortion is and what the law in the UK says about abortion.

∞ links

See pages 82–83 for more about abortion and rights.

B *The rights of a father – not recognised by the law on abortion*

C *A positive pregnancy test is not always good news*

AQA *Examiner's tip*

You need to know the meaning of the term abortion and be able to explain the current legal position in Britain with regard to it.

4.5 Rights

People who debate abortion talk about the rights of the individuals involved. This means what is morally or legally allowed. The law on abortion gives certain rights to mothers, the unborn child and the mother's existing children. However, no rights are given to the father. The father does, however, have a legal responsibility to support his children financially.

Rights of the unborn child

Those who support the rights of the unborn child say that it has a life of some sort, despite arguments about when that life begins. The foetus is dependent on the mother, but is distinct from her, and since it cannot speak for itself it needs protection. The baby is unique and deserves the same right to life as any person. If a woman voluntarily has unprotected sex, she has a responsibility to maintain the life of the resulting foetus.

Rights of the mother

Right to choose

Some people emphasise the right of a woman to choose whether or not to have a child. The foetus is in her body and it is her health, her life and her freedom that will be most affected. She must have the final say.

Right to safety

A legal abortion in early pregnancy is easy and safe – safer than childbirth. Some people argue that if women did not have to wait for two doctors to agree, abortions could be done even more quickly and safely than they are at present. They would like to see a change in the law.

Right to equality of opportunity

Every child should be a wanted child and every mother a willing mother. Supporters of abortion say abortion gives women equal opportunities in education, jobs and in society because they can decide whether and when to have children. They believe that no one knows better than the woman concerned what choices she should make in her life.

However, some supporters of women's rights oppose abortion. They think women should not be pushed into an abortion through poverty. If abortion were not so readily available, firms would have to think about more flexible working and childcare facilities for working mothers, so abortion is actually stopping progress.

Objectives

Explore the rights of those involved in a pregnancy, including the mother, the father and the unborn child.

⊂⊃ links

See pages 32–33 for the debate about when life begins.

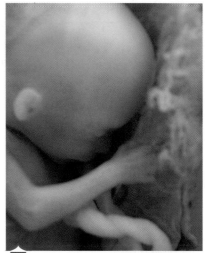

A   *What rights does the foetus have?*

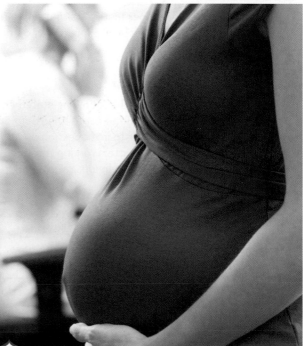

B   *What rights does the mother have?*

Fathers' rights

Fathers may feel left out in debates about abortion. Fathers have legal responsibilities for their children, but few rights. The right to make the final decision seems to lie in the woman's hands on this issue.

One situation is that the father wants the woman to have an abortion, but she wants to have the child. In this case he has no legal right to make that demand. Sometimes the father wants the mother to have the baby and she refuses. In the UK in 1987 and 2001, two fathers took the mothers of their unborn children to court to prevent them having abortions, but lost. In America, courts have consistently judged that a woman's right to an abortion cannot be vetoed by a husband or boyfriend. In fact she does not even have to tell him that she is pregnant. However, in China in 2002 a man sued his wife for denying him the right to have a child by having an abortion. Under a new equal rights law, he won his case.

C   What rights does the father have?

> 66 A woman can legally deprive a man of his right to become a parent or force him to become one against his will. 99
>
> *Armin A Brott*

Activities

1   Explain the statement, 'If a woman voluntarily has unprotected sex, she has a responsibility to maintain the life of the resulting foetus.' Do you agree with this statement? Give reasons.

2   Why do supporters of abortion say that abortion gives women equality of opportunity?

3   With a partner or in a small group, decide whether you think fathers should have the right to stop a woman from having an abortion. Explain your reasons.

Discussion activity

1   Discuss the following statements. After your discussion, decide what your own opinions are on these issues. Have you taken into account all the information and points of view in making your mind up? Make notes on key points that you can revise in preparation for the examination.

a   'People who are against abortion have no right to impose their opinions on other people.'

b   'If the government provided more free nurseries, women would not be forced into abortions.'

AQA *Examiner's tip*

Remember that supporters of women's rights are not always automatically supporters of abortion.

Summary

You should now be able to explain and evaluate the rights of those involved in abortion, including the mother, the father and the unborn child.

4

Religion and early life – summary

For the examination you should now be able to:

✔ explain religious ideas about the sanctity of life in relation to its preservation, the miracle of life and children being seen as a blessing and a gift

✔ discuss different views about when life begins, including at conception, the development of backbone, when the heart starts beating, at viability and at birth

✔ explain issues concerning the quality of life, including severe handicaps, unwanted children, poverty and suffering

✔ describe and explain the law on abortion including the 1967 and 1990 Acts

✔ discuss pro-life and pro-choice arguments and pressure groups

✔ explain key religious teachings on which religious attitudes towards abortion are based

✔ explain the reasons used by religious believers for and against abortion based on these teachings

✔ discuss the rights of those involved, such as the mother, the father, other existing children and the unborn child

✔ explain the alternatives to abortion, such as keeping the child, adoption and fostering

✔ evaluate religious attitudes and responses to abortion, using religious texts, teachings and arguments where appropriate.

AQA
Examiner's tip   Remember that you may refer to one or more than one religion or denomination in your answers.

Sample answer

1 Write an answer to the following examination question.

'The mother, the father and the unborn child should have equal rights concerning abortion.'

Do you agree? Give reasons for your answer, showing that you have thought about more than one point of view. Refer to religious arguments in your answer.

(6 marks)

2 Read the following sample answer.

I agree that all three people involved should have equal rights as they are all human beings. Religious people might say that they are all equally loved by God. Catholics believe the foetus is a human being right from conception. However, it is the woman's body. She has more right

to say what happens to her than the father does. If it came to a choice between the baby's right to life versus the mother's right to life, I think the mother's rights are more important, especially if she has other children. Muslims would agree with this as they accept abortion if the mother's life is in danger.

3 With a partner, discuss the sample answer. Do you think that there are other things that the student could have included in the answer?

4 What mark would you give this answer out of six? What are the reasons for the mark you have given? Look at the mark scheme in the Introduction on page 7 (AO2) to help you make a decision.

Fathers' rights

Fathers may feel left out in debates about abortion. Fathers have legal responsibilities for their children, but few rights. The right to make the final decision seems to lie in the woman's hands on this issue.

One situation is that the father wants the woman to have an abortion, but she wants to have the child. In this case he has no legal right to make that demand. Sometimes the father wants the mother to have the baby and she refuses. In the UK in 1987 and 2001, two fathers took the mothers of their unborn children to court to prevent them having abortions, but lost. In America, courts have consistently judged that a woman's right to an abortion cannot be vetoed by a husband or boyfriend. In fact she does not even have to tell him that she is pregnant. However, in China in 2002 a man sued his wife for denying him the right to have a child by having an abortion. Under a new equal rights law, he won his case.

C   *What rights does the father have?*

> 66 *A woman can legally deprive a man of his right to become a parent or force him to become one against his will.* 99
>
> Armin A Brott

Activities

1   Explain the statement, 'If a woman voluntarily has unprotected sex, she has a responsibility to maintain the life of the resulting foetus.' Do you agree with this statement? Give reasons.

2   Why do supporters of abortion say that abortion gives women equality of opportunity?

3   With a partner or in a small group, decide whether you think fathers should have the right to stop a woman from having an abortion. Explain your reasons.

Discussion activity

1   Discuss the following statements. After your discussion, decide what your own opinions are on these issues. Have you taken into account all the information and points of view in making your mind up? Make notes on key points that you can revise in preparation for the examination.

a   'People who are against abortion have no right to impose their opinions on other people.'

b   'If the government provided more free nurseries, women would not be forced into abortions.'

AQA Examiner's tip

Remember that supporters of women's rights are not always automatically supporters of abortion.

Summary

You should now be able to explain and evaluate the rights of those involved in abortion, including the mother, the father and the unborn child.

Introduction

The issue of abortion is fiercely debated by those in favour (**pro-choice**) and those against (**pro-life**). Each side has its own **pressure groups**. One of the key issues is the point at which life really begins. The arguments are explored below.

Pro-choice

Pro-choice arguments include:

- People in favour of abortion use the expression: 'a woman's right to choose'. The woman carries the baby and gives birth, and she will have to look after the child if it is born. She should have the right to end her pregnancy if she wishes.

- Life does not really start until the baby is born, or at the earliest, when the foetus is viable. The woman is a person already with greater rights.

- The risk to the mother's health outweighs the rights of the baby.

- The woman's circumstances should be considered. Rape victims should not be constantly reminded of their ordeal. A girl should not have to give up her education because she is pregnant. A woman deserted by the father of the child might not be able to cope on her own, emotionally or financially. A pregnancy at the wrong time could ruin a woman's career and affect her mental health. Poverty and quality of life should be taken into account.

- Adoption may be put forward as an alternative to abortion, but it is not emotionally easy for a mother to give up a baby.

- If the law changes to forbid abortion, dangerous illegal abortions will return.

- It is cruel to bring a severely physically or mentally handicapped child into the world.

- The world already has too many people, why bring unwanted children into it?

Pressure group

Abortion Rights is a national campaign group that defends safe, legal abortion and opposes any lowering of the 24-week time limit. It wants abortion to be legally available to women when they request it (known as 'abortion on demand'). It campaigns for equal access to abortion so that every woman, wherever they live, can get an abortion immediately.

Pro-life

Pro-life arguments include:

- Some opponents of abortion think that medical evidence supports their views that the unborn child is a separate human being with feelings and intelligence from conception. Therefore, abortion is murder.

Objectives

Explore pro-life and pro-choice arguments and abortion-related pressure groups.

Key terms

Pro-choice: in favour of a woman's right to choose an abortion.

Pro-life: opposed to abortion; in favour of the life of the foetus.

Pressure groups: collections of people outside government who campaign for changes in society.

links

For the debate on when life begins see pages 76–77.

links

For more about adoption see pages 92–93.

A   *Pro-choice campaigners*

- Depression and guilt may follow an abortion, which can leave mental and physical scars.
- Disabled people can enjoy a happy, fulfilled life, and would choose life over termination.
- Unwanted children could be adopted by those unable to have their own.
- The United Nations Declaration of the Rights of the Child states that children need protection both before and after birth.
- Each person is unique and has something to offer in their life.
- Abortion can be used selfishly to avoid responsibilities. It might be used thoughtlessly instead of contraception or for social reasons.

B *Pro-life campaigners*

Pressure group

The Society for the Protection of Unborn Children (SPUC) argues against abortion. It believes abortion should only be allowed when the mother's life is in danger. It campaigns for more support for pregnant mothers, increased welfare benefits for single mothers and adoption. It opposes amendments to the Human Fertilisation and Embryology Act that could reduce the number of doctors to one, allow nurses and midwives to perform abortions, and make abortion easier.

AQA Examiner's tip

The arguments in this topic are moral rather than religious ones. While religious people do use moral arguments in debates about abortion, try to use specifically religious arguments in your examination if you are asked what religious people believe.

∞links

For religious views on abortion see pages 86–91.

Activities

1. Choose what you believe to be the three strongest arguments on each side of the debate and explain why you think they are convincing. Be objective, even if you do not agree with them.

2. Should the abortion law be changed to make it easier or more difficult to obtain an abortion? Consider the time limits, the circumstances in which it is allowed, and whether two doctors are needed. Explain your opinions.

Discussion activity

1. Divide into three groups, with each group discussing one of the following statements, considering all points of view. Each group should then report back to the class on the discussion. Make notes on key points in each of the reports that you can revise in preparation for the examination.
   a 'The rights of the child are as important as the rights of the mother.'
   b 'Abortion discriminates against disabled people.'
   c 'Women are using abortion as a form of contraception now.'

Extension activity

Using the discussions and research you have conducted, prepare a class debate on the motion:

'This house believes that it is every woman's right to choose whether or not to terminate a pregnancy.'

Make up your own mind, and make sure that you can back up your opinion with facts and arguments by recording the key points of the debate. Save your notes to use when preparing for the examination.

Research activity

Using the internet or a library, find out more about the two pressure groups described in this section – see Links. Record your findings to use as an example in your examination.

Summary

You should now be able to explain pro-choice and pro-life arguments about abortion and describe the work of a pressure group on either side of the debate.

∞links

Find out more at:
www.abortionrights.org.uk
www.spuc.org.uk

■ Christianity

All Christians share a belief in the sanctity of life. Children are created in the image of God (Genesis 1:27) and are a blessing, a precious gift from God. Roman Catholics and other Christians believe that life begins at conception.

Beliefs and teachings

From the time the ovum is fertilized, a new life is begun which is neither that of the father nor of the mother… It would never become human if it were not human already.

The Roman Catholic Declaration on Procured Abortion, 1974

Abortion is deliberate killing and breaks the commandment: 'you shall not murder' (Exodus 20:13). God loves children (Matt 18:10 and Luke 18:15–16).

Beliefs and teachings

Life must be protected with the utmost care from the moment of conception: abortion and infanticide are abominable crimes.

Gaudium et Spes 51, Second Vatican Council

Before birth, God has given every person a purpose in life (Galatians 1:15). Abortion goes against God's plan for that individual. An early Christian text, called the Didache, is anti-abortion.

Beliefs and teachings

You shall not kill an unborn child, or murder a newborn infant.

Didache

Some Christians accept abortion under certain circumstances. Many Methodists and Anglicans think that sometimes abortion may be the lesser of two evils, such as in the case of rape or risk to the mother's life. The golden rule of Christianity is 'love your neighbour as yourself' (Mark 12:33). In these circumstances they ask, 'what is the most loving and compassionate thing to do?'

■ Islam

Muslims believe that all human life is precious, a sacred gift from Allah (Qur'an 17:33). Anyone who carries out an abortion will suffer in the next life.

Beliefs and teachings

No severer of womb-relationship ties will ever enter paradise.

Hadith

Many Muslims believe that life begins at the moment of conception and so an abortion is murder. There is no exception made for severely

Objectives

Explore religious teachings and beliefs about abortion in Christianity, Islam and Judaism.

⦾⦾ links

For the arguments used by religious believers when they apply these teachings to the issue of abortion see pages 90–91.

A *'Let the little children come to me… for the kingdom of heaven belongs to such as these.' (Matthew 19:14)*

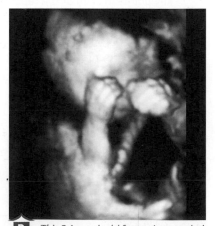

B *This 24-week old foetus is regarded as ensouled by Muslims, but there are different views on foetuses less than 120 days old*

disabled foetuses. On Judgement Day, aborted children will ask why they were killed (Qur'an 81: 7–9,11,14). Other Muslims say that the foetus is 'ensouled' (receives a soul) at 120 days. It is then regarded as a person. Before that time the mother has more rights than the foetus, but after ensoulment the mother and child have equal rights. Abortion for social and economic reasons is forbidden.

Beliefs and teachings

You shall not kill your children for fear of want. We will provide for them and for you. To kill them is a grievous sin.

Qur'an 17:31

Beliefs and teachings

...existence has stages. The first stages of existence are the settling of the semen in the womb and its mixing with the secretions of the woman. It is then ready to receive life. Disturbing it is a crime. When it develops further and becomes a lump, aborting it is a greater crime. When it acquires a soul and its creation is completed, the crime becomes more grievous. The crime reaches a maximum seriousness when it is committed after the foetus is separated (from the mother) alive.

Al-Ghazali 1982:74

◼ Judaism

God creates life and knows us even before our birth.

Beliefs and teachings

For you created my inmost being; you knit me together in my mother's womb... My frame was not hidden from you when I was made... When I was woven together ... your eyes saw my unformed body.

Psalms 139:13, 15–16

God may give us our vocation in life before birth (Isaiah 49:5 and Jeremiah 1:5). The sanctity of each individual's life is important and Jews take seriously God's command to have many children (Genesis 1:28). Abortion on demand is considered wrong. Unlike many religions, Judaism teaches that the foetus is not a person until its head is born. Therefore the mother's life has priority over that of the foetus. If a woman in labour has a life-threatening difficulty, the Talmud recommends an abortion.

Research activity

Using the internet or a library, look up the references to sacred texts or statements from religious authorities mentioned on these pages. Create a table with three columns. Put the reference in one, the text in the next, and in the final column write out what the text means in relation to abortion. Save your table to refer to when revising.

Summary

You should now be able to explain religious teachings about abortion from Christianity, Islam and Judaism.

Discussion activity

1   Consider which of these statements you think religious people might agree with most and why?

a   'Abortion should never be necessary in a loving family.'

b   'If abortion is legal, it must be all right.'

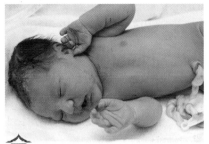

C   *Jews believe a newborn baby is a person in its own right*

Activities

1   Explain differences between the Roman Catholic and Methodist views about abortion.

2   Read the quotation by the 12th-century imam Al-Ghazali on the right of this page.

a   Explain what you think it shows about the Muslim view on abortion.

b   Which parts of this 12th-century text sound inaccurate to modern readers? Which parts could have been written by a Muslim today?

3   Explain what advice a Jewish person might give to a woman who was considering abortion.

AQA   Examiner's tip

Bear in mind, the Muslim idea of 'ensoulment' at 120 days does not mean that Muslims can have abortions before that time for just any reason. There still has to be a serious reason for ending a pregnancy.

Buddhism

For Buddhists, life is a continuous cycle of birth, death and rebirth until nibbana is reached. When conception occurs, life has already begun, so abortion is the deliberate taking of life. This goes against the first precept of 'I will not harm any living thing.'

Tibetan Buddhists say that because it is so rare to be reborn in a human form, to end this precious human rebirth wastes all the previous lives spent trying to gain enlightenment (see the case study on page 75).

However, Buddhists consider motives very important. If a person has an abortion for selfish reasons, out of despair or hatred, then it will produce bad karma. However, there are circumstances in which abortion may be the most compassionate action.

Beliefs and teachings

Abortion is the same as taking the life of a living being and as such is not a just action. However, there may be exceptional situations... if the child will be born with severe abnormalities or where the mother's life is in danger. It depends on the intention behind the action.

The Dalai Lama

Each case should be decided on its merits and wise or skilful actions taken. If the motive is selfless compassion for others, the taking of a life is balanced by good intention.

Hinduism

Brahman, the Supreme Spirit, is within every living being and all beings are part of Brahman. Therefore, all life is sacred and needs to be valued and respected.

Beliefs and teachings

In him all things exist, from him all things originate. He has become all. He exists on every side. He is truly the all.

Mahabharata Shanti Parva 47–56

Hindus believe the soul is part of the cycle of birth, death and rebirth until it is finally released. When someone dies, the soul is reborn in another person, or lesser life form. So life continues at conception. The baby is considered to be an individual from then on. Abortion destroys life that is part of God's Creation and goes against the principle of non-violence.

Beliefs and teachings

His being is the source of all being, the seed of all things that in this life have their life... He is God, hidden in all things, the inmost soul who is in all. He watches the works of creation, lives in all things, watches all things.

Svetasvatara Upanishad

A *The Buddhist wheel of samsara represents the continuous cycle of life*

B *The Dalai Lama*

A Hindu's main duty at the householder stage of life is to have children. The scriptures regard abortion as a serious sin. Abortion affects the karma of those involved, and if the motives are selfish, bad karma will result.

■ Sikhism

Sikhs believe in the sanctity of life, and that a child is a gift from God (Guru Granth Sahib 1239). Everyone may have different abilities, personalities and circumstances in their lives, but they are all important and valuable.

Beliefs and teachings

God is one and we are all his children.

Guru Granth Sahib 611

Each person has a 'divine spark'. The soul is part of God and will be reabsorbed into God when it is free from the cycle of rebirths. Human life is the highest form of life on earth and begins at conception. Therefore abortion is seen as morally wrong. Life needs to be protected.

Beliefs and teachings

Abortion is taboo as it is an interference in the creative work of God.

Mansukhani 1986b:183

Sikhs do accept abortion in certain circumstances, for example in the case of rape or if the mother's life is in danger. They believe it is up to the parents to make the right decision.

C   *Newly baptised Sikhs are told not to associate with those who practice infanticide*

Summary

You should now be able to explain religious teachings about abortion from Buddhism, Hinduism and Sikhism.

Activities

1 Give three examples of abortion based on what you see as selfish motives. Explain why you consider these cases to be selfish.

2 Explain why Hindus oppose abortion.

3 Explain what Sikhs mean when they say there is a 'divine spark' in everyone.

Research activity

Using the internet or a library, look up the references to sacred texts or statements from religious authorities on these pages and record them for use in the discussion activity and revise them for your examination. Put them in a table for easy reference, with three columns: reference, quote and meaning.

Discussion activity

Discuss the following statement in groups.

'Religious people are more concerned about the sanctity of the baby's life than about the quality of the mother's life.'

Try to draw on religious texts and teachings in your answer, and to address all different points of view. Make a note of the texts and other points raised that you find convincing, and draw on this information if you are asked to write your opinion about this issue in the examination.

AQA   *Examiner's tip*

When describing religious attitudes towards abortion, try to refer to the teachings on which they are based as evidence. Referring to the text or quoting it shows the examiner 'sound knowledge'.

4.9 Applying religious teachings to real-life situations

Buddhism

Most Buddhists oppose abortion, but some agree with the Dalai Lama that individuals' situations should be taken into account. If a mother could die, the foetus would probably be lost. Loving kindness and compassion should be the basis for decisions. Abortion may be in the baby's best interests if it will be born severely disabled. Some Japanese Buddhists make offerings and dedicate statues to Bodhisattva Jizosana to lessen their feelings of guilt if they have had an abortion.

Christianity

Christians agree abortion is wrong, but differ about whether it should be allowed in some situations.

Roman Catholics and some Christians totally oppose abortion. Every life has equal value, so abortion for severe disability is wrong. It is not up to us to judge 'usefulness'. In the case of rape, why should the child suffer for the sin of its father?

Other Christians, including many Anglicans argue that compassion is needed when judging situations. Abortion is justified to save a mother's life or in the case of rape. Abortions after 24 weeks should only occur if the child would die soon after birth. Before 24 weeks, most would accept abortions for a severely disabled child if the mother felt it was in the child's best interests. It is a matter for her conscience.

Methodists allow abortion for these cases: risk to the life or health of the mother and her existing family, great poverty, severe disability and rape.

Hinduism

Despite strong disapproval among Hindus, abortion was made legal in India in 1971. Most accept abortion to save the mother's life. Some Hindus accept abortion for rape, disability, risks to the mother's health and in circumstances of great poverty. Selfish motives, such as an unwanted pregnancy or social reasons, are condemned. Many pregnancies are ended in India when scans show the baby will be a girl, because male children are more highly valued.

Activities

1. Explain how religious people use the idea of 'compassion' when considering abortion.

2. Explain the different Christian views about when or if abortion should be allowed.

3. Why do most religions accept rape as a circumstance when abortion may be justified?

A *Sons are more highly valued than daughters in some Hindu communities*

Islam

Although abortion is forbidden, it is allowed at any time to save the mother's life as the lesser of two evils. Some scholars think it is wrong, but should not always be punished. Scholars disagree about when ensoulment takes place. Some say the embryo has rights from conception. In 1990 the Islamic World League accepted abortion before 120 days for severe disability. Some scholars allow abortion in case of rape or incest since a mother should not be made to suffer because of her child. Others argue that the right to life does not depend on the cause of the pregnancy. All scholars condemn abortion because of poverty.

Judaism

Abortion is only permitted for serious reasons and after consultation with a rabbi. Orthodox rabbis permit abortion if the mother's life is at risk from pregnancy or because she might consider suicide. Most rabbis do not accept abortion for disability and do not approve of testing for it. Other rabbis do allow abortion for disability because they are concerned for the mother's health.

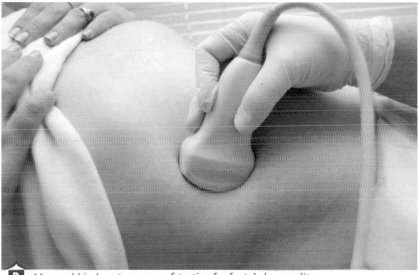

B *Many rabbis do not approve of testing for foetal abnormality*

Sikhism

Sikh scripture bans the killing of female babies. This used to happen because sons carried on the family name, did not require dowries when they married, and were expected to look after their parents. Many Sikhs extend this ban to abortion, especially of female embryos. Sikhs accept abortion to save the mother's life, and some allow it in the case of rape. Severe physical or mental disability is not seen as sufficient reason, although parents have the right to make their own decision.

links

For an explanation of ensoulment, see pages 86–87.

Discussion activity

1   In pairs, discuss one of the following statements, using religious teachings.

a   'It is right to abort a severely disabled foetus.'

b   'Testing for disability or the sex of the child should be banned.'

Make notes of the main points. Then get together with a pair who considered the other statement and make presentations to each other, summing up the discussion, the texts you referred to, and your own views. Make notes to use for revision for the examination.

AQA Examiner's tip

Remember that the official teaching of a religion may not be accepted by all believers in that faith. The decision may have to come down to a person's conscience.

Summary

You should now be able to explain how religious believers apply the teachings of their religion to situations when abortion may be considered.

4.10 Alternatives to abortion

Many religious people would wish to support a woman who has an unwanted pregnancy by offering her alternatives to abortion. Three main alternatives are explored below.

■ Keeping the baby

In the past, unmarried pregnant women were looked down upon. In most cases they were expected to give the child up for adoption. Now the social shame of being an unwed mother is not so strong. Single mothers receive help with housing and social security benefits. The father is legally required to pay a contribution to the child's support, and a young woman may receive help from her own family.

Case study

Cardinal Thomas Winning of Glasgow (1925–2001)

Cardinal Thomas Winning campaigned against abortion, but felt the Catholic Church needed to help, rather than condemn, young women who were faced with an unplanned pregnancy.

'Whatever worries or cares you may have … we will help you. If you want help to cope with raising the baby on your own … If you want to discuss adoption of your unborn child … If you need financial assistance, or help with equipment for your baby and feel financial pressures will force you to have an abortion … we will help you. If you cannot face your family, or if pressure in your local area is making you consider abortion, come to us, we will help find you somewhere to have your baby surrounded by support and encouragement…come to us, we will help you.'

■ Adoption

Most **adoptions** take place within a family, where relatives or step-parents adopt and raise a child as their own. Other adoptions are by people who cannot have a family of their own or who wish to have more children. The law requires the parents' circumstances to be fully investigated to check they can give the baby the love and care it needs. Adopted children are entitled to their birth certificates and adoption records at age 18, and may try to find out about their birth parents if they have not had contact with them before.

Religious views on adoption

Most religions follow the adoption laws of the country in which the believers live, so customs vary. Some religions restrict adoptions to children of the same religion. Muslims believe blood ties are important. If a Muslim raises a child who is not their own, they do not adopt the child. The child remains a member of its original family, even if it is brought up with all the love and care of a natural son or daughter. This is more like fostering.

Objectives

Explore the alternatives to abortion, including keeping the child, adoption and fostering.

Understand religious views on these alternatives.

Activity

1. Read the case study. With a partner or in a small group, decide whether you think the support offered by the Roman Catholic Church might change a young woman's decision about abortion.

Fostering

Fostering is when a mother places her child in temporary foster care until she is in a position to look after her child herself. Foster parents are paid by the government to look after a child within their own family. 'Looked-after children' may stay a short time or longer if the situation requires. Some are eventually adopted by their foster parents or another family.

A Adoption is when children are taken into a new family

Activity

2 Explain the difference between adoption and fostering.

Research activity

Using the internet (see Links) or a library, find out more about a religious adoption agency in the UK or an agency that had a religious origin, like Barnardos, the Catholic Children's Society, Norwood (a Jewish agency) or Adoption Matters Northwest (a Church of England adoption agency). Make notes on the work the agency does and explain how it is connected to religious teachings and beliefs. You may be able to use these examples in the examination.

links

Find out more at:

www.barnardos.org.uk

www.cabrini.org.uk

www.norwood.org.uk

www.adoptionmattersnw.org

Discussion activity

1 Choose one of the following statements to discuss with a partner.

a 'Adoption is better than abortion.'

b 'Supporting single mothers encourages irresponsible sex.'

Together, write a two-minute presentation on the issue, including reference to more than one point of view and some religious teachings. Take turns to make your presentations to the rest of the class and make notes to refer to if you are asked about this issue in the examination.

AQA Examiner's tip

You need to be able to explain the difference between adoption and fostering and give your own views on the relative merits of the three alternatives to abortion given here.

Summary

You should now be able to explain religious views on the alternatives to abortion, including keeping the child, adoption and fostering.

4

Religion and early life – summary

For the examination you should now be able to:

✔ explain religious ideas about the sanctity of life in relation to its preservation, the miracle of life and children being seen as a blessing and a gift

✔ discuss different views about when life begins, including at conception, the development of backbone, when the heart starts beating, at viability and at birth

✔ explain issues concerning the quality of life, including severe handicaps, unwanted children, poverty and suffering

✔ describe and explain the law on abortion including the 1967 and 1990 Acts

✔ discuss pro-life and pro-choice arguments and pressure groups

✔ explain key religious teachings on which religious attitudes towards abortion are based

✔ explain the reasons used by religious believers for and against abortion based on these teachings

✔ discuss the rights of those involved, such as the mother, the father, other existing children and the unborn child

✔ explain the alternatives to abortion, such as keeping the child, adoption and fostering

✔ evaluate religious attitudes and responses to abortion, using religious texts, teachings and arguments where appropriate.

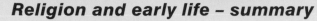

AQA Examiner's tip Remember that you may refer to one or more than one religion or denomination in your answers.

Sample answer

1 Write an answer to the following examination question.

'The mother, the father and the unborn child should have equal rights concerning abortion.'

Do you agree? Give reasons for your answer, showing that you have thought about more than one point of view. Refer to religious arguments in your answer.

(6 marks)

2 Read the following sample answer.

I agree that all three people involved should have equal rights as they are all human beings. Religious people might say that they are all equally loved by God. Catholics believe the foetus is a human being right from conception. However, it is the woman's body. She has more right

to say what happens to her than the father does. If it came to a choice between the baby's right to life versus the mother's right to life, I think the mother's rights are more important, especially if she has other children. Muslims would agree with this as they accept abortion if the mother's life is in danger.

3 With a partner, discuss the sample answer. Do you think that there are other things that the student could have included in the answer?

4 What mark would you give this answer out of six? What are the reasons for the mark you have given? Look at the mark scheme in the Introduction on page 7 (AO2) to help you make a decision.

AQA Examination-style questions

1   Look at the photograph below and answer the following questions.

(a) What is adoption?   *(1 mark)*

(b) Give two situations in which abortion is legal in Britain.   *(2 marks)*

(c) 'Life does not begin until birth.' What do you think? Explain your opinion.   *(3 marks)*

(d) Explain why some religious believers are against abortion. Refer to religious
     teaching in your answer.   *(6 marks)*

(e) 'It is right to abort an unwanted baby.'
     Do you agree? Give reasons for your answer, showing that you have thought
     about more than one point of view. Refer to religious arguments in your answer.   *(6 marks)*

5 Religion, war and peace

5.1 The causes of war

Conflict

Conflict – or state of discord or war – occurs when people's ideas, interests, values or personalities clash and when they cannot agree with each other. Conflict often refers to fighting that has been going on for some time. When countries disagree and cannot settle their differences by peaceful means, they sometimes resort to armed conflict or war.

Why do people go to war?

- To defend their country against attack.
- To defend their beliefs, religion, freedom and way of life, or sometimes to extend these to other people, for example, by imposing their values on another country.
- To defend an ally or protect a weaker country that was unfairly attacked.
- To remove their own leader or government (civil war).
- To gain more land or regain territory lost in a previous war.
- To gain wealth, power or important resources, such as oil.
- To stop atrocities such as genocide (mass murder) in another country or to depose a dictator (force a dictator to give up power).

The Vietnam War

From 1959 to 1975 a war took place in Vietnam, in Southeast Asia. The Communist government of North Vietnam, supported by other Communist countries, fought against the government of South Vietnam, supported by the USA and others. Despite the superior equipment and power of the USA, the North won the war. The communists then reunified Vietnam and took over Laos and Cambodia. Besides the many millions killed in the conflict, the war created a massive problem of refugees. The refugees, often known as 'boat people', fled to South Vietnam, Laos and Cambodia when the conflict ended. They risked death in boats that were not seaworthy to get away.

The Falklands conflict

The Falkland Islands and South Georgia are British territories off the coast of South America. For a long time, Argentina has claimed that the islands belong to them. In April 1982, Argentina invaded the Falklands and South Georgia to take them over. Britain sent a taskforce to protect the islanders and regain control of the islands, and Argentina surrendered in June 1982. The 'war' had not been officially declared and was over in 74 days. However, 907 people lost their lives.

Objectives

Introduce the causes of war and some examples of recent conflicts.

A *Why do people go to war?*

∞ links

For more on refugees, see pages 108–109.

B *Millions of soldiers and civilians died in the Vietnam War*

Consequences of war

Some consequences of war are positive. Freedom from an occupying power (a foreign country that has taken over the government), or the replacement of a corrupt government with something better can bring benefits to a country's people.

However, the main consequences of war are negative. Conflict causes deaths and injuries among both members of the armed forces and civilians. In addition, there is the destruction of a country's economy, culture and infrastructure (its roads, water supplies, electricity, schools, etc.). Disease and famine can spread when fresh water supplies have been contaminated, and homeless refugees are often reduced to living in camps in squalid conditions. The cost of conflict is enormous. Every hour £100 million is spent worldwide on weapons of war – money that could go towards solving problems of world poverty and hunger.

C   *Could the money spent on weapons of war be used better?*

Research activities 🔍

Using the internet (see Links) or a library, find out where wars are happening around the world today. Choose one conflict and find out as much as you can about why it is being fought and how it is affecting people in that place. You may be able to use it as an example in the examination.

Activities

1   Look at the causes of war listed at the start of this section. Which reasons are justifiable in your opinion?

2   Make notes on the Vietnam War and the Falklands conflict so that you can use them as examples in your examination.

3   Using your research into wars in the world today, explain whether you think the war you researched in detail is justifiable from your point of view.

Discussion activity ▪▪▪

1   In pairs or groups, discuss one of the following statements. Be sure to consider two different points of view. Make notes that you can refer to when revising for the examination. You may wish to review your discussion when you have considered religious teachings on war and peace later in this chapter, and add to your notes.

a   'Wars create more problems than they solve.'

b   'Some wars are necessary to bring about a greater good.'

Summary

You should now be able to explain the causes of war and be able to discuss an example of a recent conflict.

🔗 links

Find out more at:

http://www.globalsecurity.org (click on military> operations>world at war)

http://en.wikipedia.org (search for 'ongoing conflicts')

http://militaryhistory.about.com (click on 'current conflicts')

http://news.bbc.co.uk (search for 'war special reports')

D   *Are there any justifiable causes for war?*

AQA   Examiner's tip

You need to be able to discuss an example of a recent war and form an opinion on whether or not that particular war is justified from a religious perspective.

Peace, justice and the sanctity of life

Peace

Many people in the UK take **peace** for granted. It has been over 60 years since World War II. Most recent wars, for example in the Falklands, Afghanistan and Iraq, have been fought far away from these shores. The conflict in Northern Ireland is the exception, but since there has been a cease fire and a real effort on the part of all the parties to work together, people there have begun to appreciate the value of peace. People there might sympathise with the views of this resident of Sarajevo, Bosnia when the war in that country finally ended.

> *When they talk about peace on the TV it's big things. It's who controls what and who governs whom. But for us peace is the little things. It's going shopping, meeting your friends for a drink, fetching a newspaper without fear of being shot at by snipers in the next street. Peace means sleeping soundly in your bed... .*
>
> Sarajevo resident

Peace is not just the absence of conflict. Real peace involves a feeling of wellbeing. Even in times of conflict, many people may find inner peace, happiness and security through their religious faith. This sense of peace is a constant presence in their lives, which they may encourage through prayer and meditation. Being at peace with oneself brings a calmness and tranquillity that helps a person to avoid quarrels with others.

B *Inner peace through prayer and meditation*

Justice

Some people would say that without **justice** there can never be peace. Unfairness makes people angry and this can lead to conflict with those who are seen to be the cause of the unfairness. Real peace only exists when people are able to live in freedom with full human rights, including the right to follow a religion without fear and threats from others. Mahatma Gandhi and Martin Luther King believed that if a society oppressed its people, even if it was not involved in violence or war, it was not a peaceful society.

The wish to make up for wrongdoings is often used as a justification for going to war. However, Gandhi and King showed that it was possible to achieve justice using non-violent methods rather than armed conflict.

Objectives

Explore the concepts of peace, justice and sanctity of life in relation to war and peace.

Key terms

Peace: an absence of conflict which leads to happiness and harmony.

Justice: bringing about what is right, fair, according to the law or making up for what has been done wrong.

A *War damage in Sarajevo*

C *Lady Justice statue, showing the scales of justice*

links

To read more about Gandhi and King, see pages 66–69.

■ The sanctity of life

The **sanctity of life**, the idea that all human life is precious and should not be destroyed, is the basis for religious attitudes towards war and peace. If life is God-given and sacred, and it is not up to humans to take it away, how can religious believers justify killing people in a war?

Some believers think violence is never justified even in the pursuit of justice. This belief is called 'pacifism'. Christian pacifists believe that human beings should work for justice, but that this cannot be achieved through violence. Other religious believers disagree. Although they accept the sanctity of life, they balance it against justice and the long-term search for peace. In some cases, the sanctity of the enemies' lives is less important than establishing peace for all. In some situations, believers accept war as less of an evil than doing nothing, and the only way of establishing true peace.

Key terms

Sanctity of life: life is sacred because it is God-given.

∞ links

For more on the sanctity of life see pages 102–103 and for pacifism see pages 100–101.

PeaceMaker

PeaceMaker started in 1997 in Oldham. Some young British Asians decided to do something about the racial separation that could lead to violence in divided local communities. They wanted to challenge racism and build an inclusive, multicultural society by giving young people the chance to meet and befriend people from different ethnic groups. PeaceMaker now runs programmes that help schools, youth clubs, and workplaces build bridges that allow cultural diversity to flourish.

all people, all communities

D *The PeaceMaker logo*

Case study

Activities

1 Explain the meaning of the terms 'peace', 'justice' and 'sanctity of life' in the context of war and peace.

2 Explain how religious believers try to develop peace in their own lives.

3 Someone once said, 'There is no way to peace; peace is the way.' Explain what you think they may have meant.

4 Read the case study. Why do you think the group chose the name 'PeaceMaker'? How important is it for young people from different backgrounds to have opportunities to do things together? How might this help avoid conflict? Explain your opinions.

∞ links

Find out more at:

www.peace-maker.co.uk

Discussion activity 👥👥

1 Choose one of the following statements and discuss it with a partner. Then get together in groups of four, with each pair having discussed a different statement. Share your thoughts and ideas, and make notes to use in revising for the examination.

a 'There is no peace without justice.'

b 'Religious people should be pacifists.'

AQA *Examiner's tip*

You may be asked for the meaning of the key terms 'peace', 'justice' and 'sanctity of life' and will need to discuss how they relate to issues of war and peace.

Summary

You should now be able to explain the concepts of peace, justice and the sanctity of life in relation to war and peace.

5.3 Pacifism

Pacifism

Pacifism is based on the belief that violence against other human beings is wrong. Pacifists think wars can never be justified so they refuse to fight in them. They are 'conscientious objectors', which means killing is against their conscience, their inner feeling of doing right or wrong. Buddhists and Christians, particularly in the Society of Friends, or **Quakers**, have strong traditions of pacifism, but not all pacifists are religious believers.

What do pacifists believe?

- For religious pacifists, the sanctity of life is important. All pacifists believe that every person is part of the human family and deserves respect.
- Killing goes against teachings in sacred writings.
- War causes suffering, bitterness, hatred, prejudice and greed. The suffering is out of proportion to the evil being fought.
- War damages the environment and wastes precious lives and resources that could be used to solve global poverty and other world problems.
- Quite often negotiation is needed in the end to settle disputes, so the loss of life will have achieved very little.
- Using violence to achieve freedom or other positive goals is sinking to the same level as the oppressor.

Christians and pacifism

Beliefs and teachings

For we no longer take sword against a nation, nor do we learn any more to make war, having become sons of peace for the sake of Jesus who is our leader.

Origen, third century CE

You have heard that it was said, "Eye for eye, and tooth for tooth." But I tell you, Do not resist an evil person. If someone strikes you on the right cheek, turn to him the other also.

Matthew 5:38–9

The early Christians practised non-violence and would not take revenge even on their persecutors. Christian pacifists today follow the example of Jesus who did not resist arrest (Matthew 26:52) and allowed himself to be crucified for love of the human race. Jesus taught his followers to live and work for peace. Christian pacifists are willing to die, but not to kill for their beliefs. They will not serve as troops, but are often willing to serve as ambulance drivers, nurses or in other non-fighting roles. During World War I and II, many pacifists were put in prison for refusing to fight.

A *Christian pacifists follow the example of Jesus*

Beliefs and teachings

Blessed are the peacemakers, for they will be called sons of God.

Matthew 5:9

Many Christian denominations have pacifist groups. The Roman Catholic group Pax Christi promotes a culture of peace and non-violence through reconciliation (forgiveness) and education. The best known Christian pacifist denomination is the Society of Friends, or Quakers. Quakers believe that every person carries the inner light of God, that there is 'that of God in everyone'.

> 66 *Let us then try what love can do: for if men did once see we love them, we should soon find they would not harm us.* 99
>
> *William Penn, Quaker*

Turning the Tide

The campaign group Turning the Tide is one way Quakers work for peace. It aims to show how cycles of conflict can be broken through negotiation and non-violent strategies. The Quaker office at the United Nations promotes the peaceful prevention and resolution of armed conflict. Quakers also work for human rights, refugees and global economic issues which they believe create injustices that lead to war.

B   *Christian pacifists follow the example of Jesus*

> 66 *We utterly deny all outward wars and strife, and fightings with outward weapons, for any end, or under any pretence whatever; this is our testimony to the whole world… We testify to the world, that the Spirit of Christ, which leads us into all truth, will never move us to fight and war against any man with outward weapons, neither for the kingdom of Christ, nor the kingdoms of the world.* 99
>
> *A Declaration from the Harmless and Innocent People of God, called Quakers presented to King Charles II in 1660.*

Activities

1. Look at what pacifists believe. Which beliefs depend on religious faith, and which could be held by people who are not religious? Explain your opinions.

2. Explain why the life and teaching of Jesus encourage some Christians to be pacifists.

3. How do some Christians put their pacifist beliefs into action?

Discussion activity 👥👥👥

Prepare a televised debate on the following motion. If possible, record the debate on a video recorder. Look at the recording and decide which side had the best arguments and which side most successfully used religious arguments to support their case. Keep a note of the key points made to use when revising for the examination.

'This house believes it is impossible to hold pacifist beliefs in today's world.'

Extension activity

Find out more about pacifist groups in other Christian denominations, such as Pax Christi, or about the Turning the Tide campaign.

Prepare a presentation of their beliefs and work, and keep your notes to refer to when preparing for the examination.

Alternatively, find out about the Friends' Ambulance Unit in World War II and prepare and keep a short talk on their work and beliefs about war.

∞ links

Find out more at:
www.paxchristi.org.uk
www.turning-the-tide.org
www.bbc.co.uk/ww2peopleswar/
stories/83/a4182383.shtml

Summary

You should now be able to explain why some religious believers are pacifists and the connection between Christianity and pacifism.

Buddhism

Peace and non-violence are central to Buddhism. Right Action, part of the Eightfold Path, requires living in harmony with others. Violence harms both the person being violent and their victim as it destroys inner peace. Buddhists follow the First Precept, 'I will not harm any living thing'. Compassion for all life makes war unacceptable. Many Buddhists would say it is better to be killed than to kill.

Theravada Buddhists teach that killing is always wrong. Anyone who kills will suffer serious consequences in this or another life, even if the intention is good. Some Mahayana Buddhists believe that although killing is wrong, it may sometimes be necessary to save others.

A *Buddhist monks attend a peace demonstration*

Hinduism

Hindus believe that good karma is built up by pursuing non-violence and by working to bring peace to the world. Reverence for life and avoiding bringing harm to others were shown in the way Mahatma Gandhi rejected the use of violence in the struggle for Indian independence. He was a man of peace.

Islam

Muslims seek a just and peaceful world. The root of the word 'Islam' means 'peace' and Muslims say 'Salaam' ('Peace be upon you') to greet each other. The Qur'an teaches that peace and reconciliation are better than fighting. Muslims should not seek revenge as it is wrong to return evil with evil. Muslims should forgive others.

Objectives

Explore the key religious teachings about peace in Buddhism, Hinduism, Islam, Judaism and Sikhism.

links

For more on the concept of peace, see pages 98–99.

Discussion activity

Some Buddhists believe that 'it is better to be killed than to kill.' In pairs, discuss this belief, trying to see more than one point of view. What is your own opinion? Make notes and revise them on your discussion for possible use in your examination.

links

For more about Gandhi see pages 66–67.

Beliefs and teachings

Come together, talk together, Let our minds be in harmony... Perfect be the union among us.

Rig Veda 10:191–2

Beliefs and teachings

Paradise is for... those who curb their anger and forgive their fellow men.

Qur'an 3:134

Judaism

For Jews, peace is the highest good, and Jews greet each other with the word 'Shalom' ('Peace be upon you'). The Talmud says three things keep the world safe: truth, justice and peace, and peace is to the Earth what yeast is to dough. Jews have suffered greatly throughout history, such as in the Holocaust, so they look forward to a time of peace as Jewish prophets foretold.

B   *Jews look forward to a time of peace in the midst of conflict*

Beliefs and teachings

(God) will judge between the nations and will settle disputes for many peoples. They will beat their swords into plowshares and their spears into pruning hooks. Nation will not take up sword against nation, nor will they train for war anymore.

Isaiah 2:4

One of the commandments says, 'You shall not murder' and the Tenakh teaches that it is important to show kindness to those who are your enemies.

Beliefs and teachings

If your enemy is hungry, give him food to eat; if he is thirsty, give him water to drink.

Proverbs 25:21

Sikhism

For Sikhs, peace is a gift of God, who is called 'a haven of peace'. Sikhs pray for the welfare of others and believe in the principle of non-violence. Guru Nanak taught that if someone hurt you, you should put up with it three times; on the fourth time God would defend you. He taught that no one should be regarded as an enemy or a foreigner, and that hate and prejudice are not possible in people who are at peace. The Guru Granth Sahib teaches Sikhs to regard others as they regard themselves and to cause no one any suffering.

C   *Guru Nanak*

Activities

1   Explain the beliefs and teachings of one religion about peace.

2   Explain the meaning of the Talmud's teaching, that peace is to the earth what yeast is to dough.

3   Do you agree with Guru Nanak that if a person has God within them, they cannot hate others? Explain your opinion.

4   Religions teach people to live in peace. Why do you think their followers do not always do this?

Research activity

Using the internet or a library, find out more about how religious people promote peace. You could try the websites given in the Links for the Buddhist Peace Fellowship, the Three Faiths Forum or the Sikh 'Akhand Jaap' 24-hour Prayer for Peace. Take notes and revise them so that you can use what you find out in your research in the examination.

links

Find out more at:
www.bpf.org
www.3ff.org.uk
www.sikhkids.com (click on 'Akhand Jaap')

AQA   *Examiner's tip*

Although you need only answer from one religion's perspective you may find it easier to answer the questions if you give two religions' teachings.

Summary

You should now be able to explain religious beliefs and teachings about peace in Buddhism, Islam, Hinduism, Judaism and Sikhism.

5.5 'Just War' and 'holy war'

Just War

Religions oppose war, but many of them believe fighting is justifiable if it is the only course of action that will prevent a real evil.

Over many years Christian thinkers developed conditions for a **Just War**. The war must:

- have a just cause (such as self-defence)
- be lawfully declared by a proper authority (that is, the rulers of the countries involved)
- have a good intention (such as to promote good and avoid evil) and once its aims are achieved it must end
- be a last resort after all other ways of resolving the problem have been tried first
- have a reasonable chance of success (it is wrong to send troops to certain death if there is no chance of winning)
- be fought by just means (anyone not fighting in the war should not be harmed) and in proportion to the aims it seeks to achieve (excessive force must not be used)
- only occur if the good achieved will outweigh the evil that led to the war.

The concept of the Just War is also present in Hinduism, Islam, Judaism and Sikhism. Buddhism does not support the idea of war, but some Buddhists have fought in self-defence.

Holy war

Most people today find the idea of a **holy war** a contradiction. Killing thousands seems far from holy. However, in ancient times people believed God was on their side and had called them to fight his enemies. In the Old Testament/Tenakh there are many accounts of battles fought under God's protection. The Crusades were seen by both Christians and Muslims as holy wars, defending places sacred to their faiths.

Holy wars have religious aims or goals. They are authorised by God or by a religious leader. Those who take part believe they will gain a spiritual reward, such as heaven or paradise. Religious leaders may declare a holy war to defend their religion or their followers who are being persecuted in another country. Some holy wars were fought to win back a country that used to follow the beliefs of a particular religion, or to spread their faith.

Christianity and war

Although Jesus taught peace, forgiveness and overcoming evil with good, he also vigorously opposed wrongdoing. On one occasion, he used force to drive out those who were turning the Temple into 'a den of thieves'. Today, the Roman Catholic Church promotes peace by working to end the causes of injustice. It condemns use of weapons of mass destruction, but recognises the right of self-defence as a last resort.

Objectives

Explore the reasons why religious believers might go to war, including the criteria (conditions) for a 'Just War' and a 'holy war'.

Understand Christian views about fighting in a war.

Key terms

Just War: a war that the Christian Church defines as acceptable: this must fit certain criteria.

Holy war: fighting for a religious cause or God probably controlled by a religious leader.

∞ links

The teachings of the other religions on 'Just War' and 'holy war' are given on pages 106–107.

A *A World War II memorial: did this war meet many of the criteria for a Just War?*

∞ links

For more on weapons of mass destruction see pages 114–115.

Some Christians have reluctantly accepted the necessity of violent action. Dietrich Bonhoeffer, a German Christian minister during World War II, took part in a plot to assassinate Hitler. He could not stand by while millions of Jews were murdered. Some South American Christians support 'liberation theology'. They accept the need for fighting to overthrow unjust, oppressive governments.

B   *The Crusades: in the 11th to 13th centuries, Christians fought what they believed to be a holy war to gain control of the holy Land from the Muslims*

Discussion activity

In pairs, discuss this statement. Remember to consider all points of view, and refer to religious beliefs in your discussion. Make notes of the main points raised and revise these in preparation for the examination.

'No war is holy.'

Research activity

Using the internet or a library, find out more about Christians who have supported the use of violence in certain circumstances. For example, Dietrich Bonhoeffer or liberation theology supporters in South America. Do you agree with the position these people have taken? Record and revise your findings so that you can use those you have researched as examples in the examination.

Summary

You should now be able to explain the reasons why some religious believers might go to war, including the criteria for a Just War and a holy war, and explain Christian views about fighting in a war in certain circumstances.

Activities

1   Explain the criteria needed for a war to be a 'Just War' according to the rules developed by Christian thinkers.

2   How likely do you think it is that a war could fit all these criteria at the same time?

3   Explain the meaning of a 'holy war'.

4   Do holy wars fit the criteria for Just Wars?

5   Think of some examples of recent wars. (You may have researched a recent conflict while studying pages 96–97 that you could reconsider here.) Do they fit the criteria of a Just War? Explain your opinions.

5.6 | Religions and war

Buddhism

Theravada Buddhists believe that killing is always wrong. Mahayana Buddhists believe that if people are motivated by love of others, for example, to save the lives of many innocent people, then killing is not necessarily wrong. However, it must be carried out unselfishly and with a willingness to accept bad spiritual consequences. Buddhist countries have armies for the sake of defence.

Hinduism

Most Hindus think war is justifiable if their country is invaded, if the lawful government has been overthrown, or if people are oppressed or exploited. War should be a last resort, have a just cause, be controlled and not cause unnecessary suffering. Unarmed civilians and people who surrender should not be killed.

Protection of the innocent is the duty of the Kshatriyas (warrior caste). Killing is fair in self-defence or to protect women and priests. In the Bhagavad Gita, Krishna tells Arjuna that he must fulfil his duty to fight. Despite his horror of war, he must act unselfishly for the good of humanity.

> ### Beliefs and teachings
>
> For a warrior, nothing is higher than a war against evil.
>
> *The Bhagavad Gita* 2:31

Islam

Muslims believe in the jihad (an Arabic word meaning 'to struggle'), or Just War. The greater jihad is the fight against temptation in their lives, and the lesser jihad is military struggle in defence of Islam, self-defence and justice. The Qur'an gives those who have been attacked permission to fight back.

A jihad or Just War must:

- be started and controlled by a religious leader
- have a just cause
- be a last resort
- keep suffering, including that of innocent civilians, to a minimum
- protect trees, crops and animals
- not be fought to gain territory or as an act of aggression
- aim to restore peace and freedom
- enable the release of all prisoners of war.

Those killed in jihad are seen as martyrs who will enter paradise.

Objectives

Explore the key religious teachings about war in Buddhism, Hinduism, Islam, Judaism and Sikhism.

⚭ links

The teachings of Christianity on war and peace are given on pages 100–105.

A *Arjuna had a duty to fight*

> ### Beliefs and teachings
>
> The person who struggles so that Allah's word is supreme is the one serving Allah's cause.
>
> *Hadith*

Judaism

In the Tenakh, God is portrayed as a warrior. Moses taught Jews to defend themselves in proportion to the offence committed against them. The struggle for the Jewish homeland made war a religious duty. There are many stories of war heroes like Joshua, Samson, King David and Gideon. However, the Code set out by Maimonides, a 12th century CE rabbi, said when siege is laid to a city, a chance for escape should be provided. Most Jews see some wars as obligatory – a necessary last resort. They are fought in self-defence, in pre-emptive strikes against an enemy about to invade, or by God's command.

Sikhism

The kirpan (sword) symbolizes the willingness of Sikhs to defend people's religious freedom, dignity and self-respect. A Just War is allowed as a last resort in self-defence or for a righteous cause, such as fighting injustice, but never for revenge. Minimum force must be used and innocent civilians must not be harmed. Enemy land or property must not be looted and must be returned when fighting ends. Only disciplined soldiers must fight, not mercenaries (soldiers hired to fight in a foreign army).

Beliefs and teachings

When all efforts to restore peace prove useless and no words avail, lawful is the flash of steel, it is right to draw the sword.

Guru Gobind Singh

B Sikhs carrying the symbolic kirpan

Activities

1 Do you think there are any circumstances in which killing might be done unselfishly? Explain your opinion.

2 Which teachings about war do most religions have in common?

3 Explain the meaning of jihad. Why do you think it is sometimes used to mean a holy war?

4 Do you think attacking another country before it attacks you is ever justified? Explain your opinions.

5 Why do you think Sikhs are against the use of mercenaries in war? Explain your opinions.

Discussion activity

1 In pairs or small groups, discuss one of the following statements. Come up with at least three arguments to support the statement and three to oppose it, drawing on religious teachings. Discuss your arguments with another group. Which do you find most convincing? What is your own opinion? Record the statements to use in your preparation for the examination.

a 'If you do not go to war for what you believe in, your enemies will think you are weak.'

b 'No war can avoid the killing of innocent people, so no war is ever just.'

Summary

You should now be able to explain why some religious people think war is justified, based on the beliefs and teachings of Mahayana Buddhism, Islam, Hinduism, Judaism and Sikhism.

AQA Examiner's tip

You need to be able to explain the circumstances in which believers from at least one religion would say that war is justified.

Victims of war

Victims of war

War has many victims besides the soldiers that are injured and killed. Survivors can have long-lasting physical and mental injuries. Cities are destroyed, homes lost, families and friends are separated and children are orphaned.

A *Landmines used in wartime can continue to cause injuries long after a conflict is over*

Trying to restore law and order is difficult when some people may want revenge on old enemies. Some people become **refugees**, fleeing to other countries with few possessions and no rights of citizenship there. They may be forced to live in refugee camps with poor conditions, and little water and food. If the neighbouring country is poor it finds it difficult to provide help for refugees.

The Red Cross and Red Crescent

Case study

The Red Cross

The Red Cross was started when Henry Dunant, a Swiss businessman, witnessed a battle in Solferino in 1859 in which 40,000 soldiers were killed or left dying on the battlefield. He was so shocked that they had no medical care, he organised the town to help. He later wrote about his experience and gathered people with military and medical experience to form a committee. His aim was to establish voluntary relief organisations and treaties to protect neutral medical staff and field hospitals on the battlefield. A conference was held in Geneva, which agreed to start national relief societies and to adopt an emblem to show the volunteer was not an 'enemy' but a neutral helper. The first Geneva Convention adopted rules to govern this and the treatment of prisoners of war.

The International **Red Cross** and **Red Crescent** Movement now has about 97 million volunteers worldwide. All members of the Movement are seen as neutral. Their aims are to protect and ensure respect for human life and health; and to prevent and alleviate suffering without any discrimination based on nationality, religion, race, class or political opinions.

Objectives

Think about the effects of war on its victims, including refugees and those maimed (injured).

Understand how organisations like the Red Cross and Red Crescent help victims of war.

Key terms

Refugees: people who flee from their homes seeking safety elsewhere.

Red Cross: a humanitarian agency that helps people suffering from war or other disasters.

Red Crescent: the same as the Red Cross. National Red Crescent Societies are found predominantly in Muslim countries.

B *Red Cross, Red Crescent and Red Crystal: emblems of neutrality and protection*

Three parts of the Movement

- The International Committee of the Red Cross (ICRC) was founded in Geneva in 1863 (see the Case study). It organises medical care for wounded soldiers, supervises treatment of prisoners of war, searches for missing people, protects civilians and can act as a neutral intermediary between the warring sides.

- Red Cross or Red Crescent societies, like the British Red Cross and the Egyptian Red Crescent. There are 186 societies in nearly every country of the world.

- The International Federation of these societies in Geneva, Switzerland. The Federation coordinates and supports their work when there is a major disaster or large-scale emergency and organises campaigns against the use of landmines.

The Movement in action

The two World Wars brought the different parts of the movement together because there were so many victims of war. The ICRC takes the lead in war situations and the Federation coordinates international disaster relief in peace time. In recent conflicts, ICRC workers have been killed in Sarajevo, Chechnya, Afghanistan and Iraq. It seems that the Red Crescent and Red Cross emblems may not be accepted as neutral by some people any more. At a diplomatic conference in 2005, States adopted an additional protective emblem, the Red Crystal emblem. Like the red cross and Red Crescent emblems, the Red Crystal emblem is a sign of neutrality and protection, and has no religious or political significance. All three emblems have the same status and meaning in international law.

Research activity

Using the internet or a library, find out how the United Nations High Commission for Refugees helps people who are fleeing from conflict. Make notes on the problems refugees face and revise them for use in the examination.

Activities

1   Explain the possible effects of war on a country and its people.

2   Explain how the International Committee of the Red Cross can protect the life and dignity of people in a war.

3   Read the case study. What made Henry Dunant form a society that became the Red Cross?

Discussion activity

'The point of war is to kill the enemy, not try to help them when they are injured.'

In pairs, discuss this statement from the point of view of the humanitarian agencies described on these pages. What arguments do you think they would use against this? Make notes of key points to use in preparation for the examination.

AQA Examiner's tip

Athough the Red Cross/Red Crescent societies are not religious organisations, despite their symbols, you should consider what religious believers would think of their work.

links

Find out more at:
www.unhcr.org

Extension activity

1   Use the websites in the Links below to find four Geneva Conventions and three Protocols (rules) for war.

   a   Make a list of the rules.

   b   Choose one and research it further by following links on the website.

2   Should there be 'rules' about war, in your opnion? How can these rules be enforced?

links

Find out more at:
www.icrc.org (search for 'Geneva conventions')
www.icrc.org (click on Humanitarian law >Treaties and customary law>International humanitarian law: the essential rules)

Summary

You should now be able to describe the effects of war on its victims including refugees and those maimed, and explain how organisations like the Red Cross or Red Crescent help victims of war.

5.8 Religious believers who have worked for peace

The Dalai Lama

Tenzin Gyatso was born in 1935 in Tibet. He was enthroned as the 14th Dalai Lama (the Buddhist spiritual leader of the Tibetan people) in 1950 in Lhasa, Tibet's capital city.

Chinese occupation of Tibet

In 1950, the Chinese army invaded Tibet. Despite peace talks and attempts to bring about a peaceful solution, the Chinese treated the Tibetan people badly. In 1959, thousands demonstrated on the streets of Lhasa, calling for the Chinese to leave. The Chinese army crushed the Tibetan National Uprising. Over 80,000 Tibetans fled the country. The Dalai Lama escaped to India, where he has lived since 1960 as leader of the Tibetan government-in-exile.

Peaceful response

As a Buddhist, the Dalai Lama refused to consider violence to win back his country. Instead, he encouraged refugees to save the Tibetan culture and way of life. Over 200 monasteries were established in India and refugee children are taught Tibetan language, history, religion and culture. In 1987, the Dalai Lama proposed a five-point peace plan, which has been rejected. He still works for a peaceful resolution and, in 1989, was awarded the Nobel Peace Prize. In his struggle for his country's freedom, he has consistently opposed the use of violence. He has urged people to find peaceful solutions based on tolerance and mutual respect to preserve the historical and cultural heritage of his people.

Activity

1 Explain why the Dalai Lama refuses to use violence to free Tibet from Chinese occupation. Use your knowledge of Buddhist teachings and beliefs to help you.

Objectives

Explore the work of religious believers who have worked for peace.

links

Martin Luther King, Desmond Tutu and Mahatma Gandhi also worked for peace through non-violent means: see pages 66–71.

A Tenzin Gyatso, the 14th Dalai Lama

B The Chinese flag flies over Potala Palace in Lhasa – the home that the exiled Dalai Lama cannot live in

AQA Examiner's tip

The choice of a religious believer who has worked for peace is yours, but remember that the person should be a known religious believer whose work resulted from their faith.

Irena Sendler

Irena Sendler was a Roman Catholic, born in 1910 in Poland. She worked as a social worker in Poland's capital city, Warsaw.

German occupation of Poland

In 1939 the Germans invaded Poland. Poles no longer ran their own country and did not enjoy human rights. Under Nazi rule, Jews were severely persecuted. They were forced to live in cramped ghettoes and wear yellow Stars of David so that they could be easily identified. Many were sent to their deaths in concentration camps.

C *Irena Sendler*

D *Many Polish Jews died in camps like this one*

> **"** *Every child saved with my help is the justification of my existence on this Earth, and not a title to glory.* **"**
>
> *Irena Sendler*

Caring response

Irena was a member of the Polish resistance, an undercover organisation working against the occupying forces. She offered Jews food and shelter, and helped create over 3,000 false documents so Jewish families could avoid arrest. It was very risky – everyone in a household could be killed if they were found to be hiding Jews.

As a social worker, she had a special permit to enter the Warsaw ghetto to check for typhus. When visiting, she wore a Star of David to show solidarity with the Jewish people. She organised the smuggling of Jewish children from the ghetto, carrying them out in boxes, suitcases or ambulances, and disguising babies as packages. The children were placed for safety with Polish families, or in Catholic convents, orphanages and priests' houses. She hid lists of their old and new names in jars.

In 1943, Irena was arrested by the Nazi secret police, severely tortured and sentenced to death. The resistance saved her by bribing German guards. She was left unconscious in the woods, with broken legs and arms, and was officially dead. From then on, she lived in hiding continuing her work for Jewish children.

When war ended, she dug up the jars with the children's identities and tried to reunite them with their families. Tragically, most of their parents had died in extermination camps. She was nominated for the Nobel Peace Prize in 2007.

Activities

2 Explain how Irena Sendler worked for peace.

3 Why would someone like Irena Sendler risk their own safety on behalf of people of a different religion?

Discussion activity

'You can achieve more by using love and peace than by using violence and hate.'

In small groups, consider how the Dalai Lama and Irena Sendler would respond to this statement. What is your own view? Refer to religious teachings in your discussion, and make notes to use in your revision for the examination.

Summary

You should now be able to describe how the Dalai Lama and Irena Sendler worked for peace.

5.9   Keeping the peace in times of terror

The United Nations

The **United Nations (UN)** was set up at the end of World War II and now has 192 member states. It seeks to persuade countries to settle their differences without fighting. Its aims are:

- to help countries cooperate with each other through international law and security
- economic development
- social progress
- the protection of human rights
- to establish world peace.

Sometimes the UN intervenes directly in a conflict. More often it sends peacekeeping forces, with troops supplied by member nations. These are placed between opposing armies, or between groups within a country where a civil war is taking place, to stop the fighting. They do their best to protect civilians and ensure aid is given where it is needed. These forces also help to keep the peace once the conflict is over. The UN has an International Court of Justice in The Hague. This court tries cases of serious crimes against humanity committed during wars and other disputes between nations.

A   *The official flag of the United Nations*

B   *What does this statue outside the UN headquarters suggest about the organisation's aims?*

NATO

The North Atlantic Treaty Organisation, or **NATO**, was created in 1949. It is a military alliance. Twenty-six countries in Europe, the USA and Canada are now members. If a NATO country is attacked, the others view it as an attack on their own nations. When NATO was started, the main threat was seen as the then Soviet Union, which formed the Warsaw Pact in 1955 with its own neighbours. There was great tension and rivalry between NATO and Warsaw Pact countries in what was known as the Cold War. Changes in global politics mean that many former Warsaw Pact countries are now part of NATO.

Research activity

2   Look up the NATO website using the web address in the Links. Then research the following and record your findings to refer to in the examination.

a   Using the link 'What is NATO?', research five key facts about the organisation.

b   Using the link 'What's new?', research two areas, conflicts or projects in which NATO is currently involved and note how it works to keep peace.

links
www.nato.int

■ Terrorism

Terrorism is the unlawful use of extreme violence, usually against innocent civilians, to achieve a political goal. The object is to achieve maximum publicity and terrify the public. Some terrorists target the government of a country that they blame for injustice or oppression, but innocent people are usually victims. Terrorists who are motivated by religion believe God will reward them for doing what they see as his will.

Most people think terrorism can never be justified because it harms innocent people and promotes fear. Others believe that on very rare occasions violence may be the only way to get the world to take notice when all other means have failed.

C   *Attack on the World Trade Center on September 11th 2001*

Research activity

3   Using the library or internet, find out about the September 11 terrorist attacks on New York. Make notes that you can refer to later on the following.

a   What happened.

b   Who carried out the attacks and why.

c   What happened after the attacks.

AQA   **Examiner's tip**

Use your knowledge of religious teachings to explain whether religious people would accept terrorism.

Discussion activity

1   With a partner or in a small group, discuss these statements. Explain your opinions, and consider what religious people would say about the issues. Make notes of key points and revise these to use in the examination.

a   'The UN is powerless to stop wars.'

b   'Terrorism is never justified.'

Summary

You should now be able to explain how the UN and NATO try to keep the peace and discuss whether terrorism is justified from a religious perspective.

Weapons of mass destruction

Weapons have developed over the centuries, from swords, to fire power, to warplanes, to the most sophisticated computer-operated missiles. Weapons continue to develop, and more and more countries want the latest, most powerful ones available.

■ Weapons of mass destruction

Weapons of mass destruction (WMD) are weapons that can kill large numbers of people at once. These include biological, chemical and nuclear weapons (Conventional weapons do not contain these).

- Biological weapons have bacteria, viruses or other infective material in them that can lead to disease or death. If these enter the food chain, water supplies or pollute the atmosphere, it would lead to illness and death on a massive scale. Although they were banned under the Geneva Conventions, they have been used since then and are still being developed by many nations.

- Chemical weapons were used in World War I, by both Britain and Germany. Despite being banned in 1925, they were used by the USA in Vietnam and by Iraq against Iran and the Kurds. They are still being manufactured and stockpiled. Different types of chemical weapons can cause choking, burning paralysis and destruction of the environment.

Objectives

Understand the meaning of weapons of mass destruction.

Explore the arguments for and against nuclear weapons and their proliferation.

Key terms

Weapons of mass destruction (WMD): weapons that can kill large numbers of people and/or cause great damage.

∞ links

For an explanation of the Geneva Conventions, see pages 108–109.

A The chemical weapon napalm was used in Vietnam

B The gas masks used by soldiers in WWI would be useless against modern-day weapons of mass destruction

- Nuclear weapons (weapons that work by nuclear reaction) cause huge devastation. Afterwards, radioactive fallout kills many more than the original explosion. America dropped two such bombs on Japan, which they claimed ended World War II more quickly, and saved lives as well as taking them. Today's nuclear weapons are even more powerful and would, if used, create a nuclear winter lasting months, and a 50 per cent increase in ultraviolet radiation. This would destroy life on Earth.

Arguments for and against nuclear weapons

Some people accept the possession of nuclear weapons even if they do not want them to be used. They say the weapons act as a deterrent: the fact that a country possesses them prevents that country from being attacked, and two countries with weapons are unlikely to attack each other. They might agree with a reduction in the numbers of weapons across many countries, but they think it would make a country vulnerable if they were disposed of altogether by that country alone.

Others are in favour of Britain getting rid of all nuclear weapons whether or not any other countries do. The Campaign for Nuclear Disarmament (CND) was set up to protest against nuclear weapons. CND believes that such weapons pose an unacceptable risk to humanity. The **proliferation** of nuclear weapons makes the chances greater that irresponsible governments or terrorists might obtain them. The destruction they would cause cannot be justified for any reason. Their use goes against all the principles of the 'Just War'. All religions oppose the use of nuclear weapons and support disarmament. Many religions have spoken out against them and in favour of negotiations to gradually eliminate them.

C   *An artist's impression of a devastating nuclear explosion*

Research activity

1   Use the ZeroNukes weblink (see Links) or a library to find out what religious groups have said about the production and use of nuclear weapons. Choose several different groups and write a short summary of their positions on this issue. Do you agree with their views? Give reasons for your opinions. Keep your notes to help you prepare for the examination.

Activities

1   Explain the different types of weapons of mass destruction: biological, chemical and nuclear. Give an example of when each type of weapon has been used.

2   Explain carefully whether religious people could ever justify using weapons of mass destruction.

3   Why might some religious people think keeping nuclear weapons as a deterrent is justified?

Research activity

2   Using the CND weblink (see Links) or a library, find out more about the Campaign for Nuclear Disarmament in the UK. Focus on its work related to weapons rather than nuclear power, and list its main aims in this area. Keep your notes to help you revise.

Summary

You should now be able to explain religious perspectives on weapons of mass destruction and the arguments for and against nuclear weapons and their proliferation.

links

Find out more at:
www.zero-nukes.org (click on 'Religious statements')

Beliefs and teachings

Nowadays, [war] is much more terrifying because a man in an office can push a button and kill millions of people and never see the human tragedy he has created. The mechanization of war... poses an increasing threat to peace.

Dalai Lama

links

Find out more at:
www.cnduk.org (click on 'About CND')

AQA *Examiner's tip*

You need to be able to apply the religious teachings and beliefs you have already considered to whether or not the use or proliferation of weapons of mass destruction is justified.

5

Religion, war and peace – summary

For the examination you should now be able to:

✔ explain the causes of war, giving examples of recent conflicts

✔ explain the concepts of peace, justice and sanctity of life in relation to war and peace

✔ explain the meaning of pacifism and the reasons why some religious believers are pacifists

✔ explain key religious teachings and modern statements about war and peace

✔ explain reasons why religious believers might go to war, including the criteria for a 'Just War' and 'holy war'

✔ discuss the effects of war on its victims, including refugees and those who are maimed, and describe the work of organisation that help them like the Red Cross and Red Crescent

✔ describe the work of a religious believer who has worked for peace

✔ describe the work of the UN, NATO and peacekeeping forces, and discuss the issue of terrorism

✔ explain the meaning of weapons of mass destruction and evaluate arguments for and against nuclear weapons and their proliferation

✔ evaluate religious attitudes and responses to war and peace, using religious texts, teachings and arguments where appropriate.

Sample answer

1 Write an answer to the following examination question.

'Using nuclear weapons in a war is never justified.'

Do you agree? Give reasons for your answer, showing that you have thought about more than one point of view. Refer to religious arguments in your answer.

(6 marks)

2 Read the following sample answer.

> I agree. Nuclear weapons should never be used because they destroy innocent civilians as well as the environment so they go against the Christian idea of a 'just war'. The radioactive fallout would affect large areas even beyond where the war was taking place. Peace might be restored, but only because no one was left to argue. On the other hand, when America dropped the atomic bomb on Japan, it did end the war quickly.

3 With a partner, discuss the sample answer. Do you think that there are other things that the student could have included in the answer?

4 What mark would you give this answer out of six? What are the reasons for the mark you have given? Look at the mark scheme in the Introduction on page 7 (AO2) to help you make a decision.

AQA Examination-style questions

1   Look at the photograph below and answer the following questions.

(a) What is meant by a 'holy war'?   *(1 mark)*

(b) Give **two** reasons why countries might go to war.   *(2 marks)*

(c) 'Religious believers should be pacifists.' What do you think? Explain your opinion.   *(3 marks)*

(d) Explain why some religious believers are prepared to fight in a war.   *(6 marks)*

(e) 'Nuclear war can never be justified.' Do you agree? Give reasons for your answer,
     showing that you have thought about more than one point of view.
     Refer to religious arguments in your answer.   *(6 marks)*

AQA
Examiner's tip   In Question (e) the statement could be argued on moral grounds without a religious
perspective. However, if you do not include a religious argument, belief or teaching, you
will achieve no more than three marks.

6.1 Birth and initiation ceremonies

Most religions have rituals to mark special occasions. This may involve **initiation** ceremonies to bless, protect or welcome a person into the faith community. The birth of a child is seen as a cause for rejoicing and most religions have ceremonies to celebrate the event, described below.

Buddhism

Buddhism does not have a special ceremony to mark the birth of a child, so local customs are usually followed. Often the child is named in the local temple. A monk sprinkles water over the baby while blessing the child for a happy life.

Christianity

Most Christians have their babies baptised as a sign of initiation into the family of the church. This involves the priest pouring water from the font on to the baby's head and declaring, 'I baptise you in the name of the Father, Son and Holy Spirit.' Promises are made on the baby's behalf by the godparents. These may be confirmed when the person is old enough to understand what they are doing. In Orthodox Christianity, the baby is immersed in water, dressed in white and oil is poured on its head (known as Chrismation). Baptism symbolises the washing away of sin and a new life as a follower of Christ. Some Christians prefer to have a service of thanksgiving where the child is blessed. Some denominations, such as Baptists, believe it is only right to be baptised when a person has made their own decision to become a Christian.

Hinduism

In Hinduism, there are several birth and initiation ceremonies. Some take place before birth to offer prayers of protection on both the mother and the unborn child. At birth, the child may be welcomed by honey being put in its mouth and the name of God being whispered in its ear. Other ceremonies include naming the child, celebrating its first trip out and marking the child's first taste of solid food. Ear-piercing and first haircut ceremonies may also be performed. The Upanayana (sacred thread) ceremony is performed when the child reaches school age. This involves wearing three strands of sacred thread to represent three vows: to respect knowledge, their parents and society.

Objectives

Investigate birth and initiation ceremonies.

Key terms

Initiation: being entered formally into a religion.

links

For more about the confirmation of these promises, see pages 130–131.

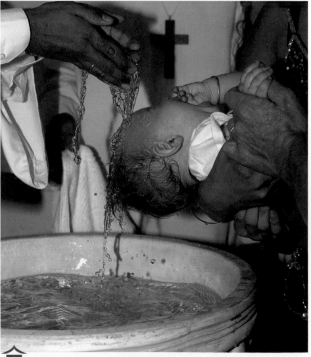

A *Priest pouring water from the font on the baby being baptised – at a Christian ceremony*

Islam

As soon as possible after birth, the father whispers the Adhan (Muslim call to prayer) in the ear of the newborn baby. This welcomes them into the Muslim community. Something sweet, such as sugar or a date, is put on the baby's tongue. Gifts are given to the poor in thanks to Allah for the new child. After seven days, the Aqiqah ceremony occurs, which involves shaving the baby's head, naming the child, and donating to the poor. For boys, after eight days Khitan (circumcision) may take place.

Judaism

Baby girls are blessed and named the first time their parents take them to the synagogue after the birth. Baby boys go through the covenant of circumcision (brit milah). This is performed by a mohel, usually on the eighth day after birth, to initiate the boy into the Jewish community. The child is now seen as religiously pure and part of God's chosen people. Family and friends then celebrate with a meal.

Sikhism

At birth, the Mool Mantar is whispered into the baby's ear and some honey is put on its tongue. Usually the child is taken to the gurdwara within 40 days of its birth. There the priest opens the Guru Granth Sahib. The family chooses a name beginning with the first letter from the page that was opened. The name is announced to the congregation and Karah Prashad (sweet food) is eaten to celebrate the entry of the child into the Sikh community.

Research activity

Use the internet or library to find out more about the birth ceremonies, described above, for the religions you are studying.

Activities

1   Explain what happens in one religion at birth and/or when a child is initiated into the religion.

2   'Initiation ceremonies are best left until a person is old enough to decide for themselves if they want to belong to a religion.' What do you think? Explain your opinion. Refer to the religions you are studying in your answer.

Discussion activity

With a partner, in a small group or as a class, discuss the value and purpose of birth and initiation ceremonies. Refer to at least one religion in your discussion, and remember to try to include a range of points of view. Make notes on key points that you can use when revising for the examination.

AQA Examiner's tip

Be prepared to describe at least one birth and initiation ceremony and explain its significance.

Summary

You should now be able to explain what happens at the birth and initiation ceremonies for the religion(s) you are studying and their significance for believers.

What influences young people?

Influences vary from person to person, depending on their circumstances and environment. Family, friends, the media, school, culture and religion may all play a part in shaping a young person's personality, decision-making and morality. All aspects of a person – their character, sense of responsibility, good and bad habits, ability to cope with difficulties, and their **spirituality** – are shaped during childhood.

Home

Someone's home and upbringing may have an enormous influence on a young person. It can be argued that the mother is the most influential person in most children's lives, followed by the father and other family members. However, sometimes the father is the main role model. If the parents are working, the grandparents may take on much of the responsibility. In the home children are taught what is acceptable behaviour. They also observe what other family members do and behaviour and attitudes are copied. If the family is religious, the child will be brought up in the beliefs, teachings, practices and rules of that religion. That may affect a person's life choices. They are likely to avoid careers that are either not valued or forbidden by their religion. Attitudes to religion, spirituality, relationships, morality and life are all learned about first of all in the home.

Religious upbringing

In some families, religion is ignored as parents are non-believers. In others, religion is central to their way of life: religious belief is passed on to the young person and rituals are observed. Prayer or meditation, sacred writings and the faith communities and their leaders are all introduced at an early age so religion becomes a natural part of the young people's lives. Religious teachings help to guide a person in life.

> ### Objectives
> Understand the influences of the home and upbringing on a person and on the decisions they take.

> ### Key terms
> **Spirituality**: a sense of something that is outside normal human experience.

A *Religion is passed on through the family*

Buddhism

In Buddhism a child will observe the worship in the home and learn to respect the shrine room with its statute of the Buddha, incense burner, candles and trays of food offerings.

Christianity

Christian families may teach their children to pray, say grace before meals, and attend worship on Sundays. Bible stories are taught and celebrations take place at festivals, such as Christmas, Pentecost and Harvest Festival.

Hinduism

Hindu children are introduced to both worship in the temple and in the home and the family god or goddess. Festivals such as Diwali and Holi will be celebrated in which children play games and have fun.

B *Holi colours*

Islam

In Islam, at the age of four years, four months and four days the Bismillah ceremony occurs. This marks the start of the child's religious education. The father encourages the child to repeat 'In the name of Allah, the Compassionate, the Merciful'. Mothers also train their children, often while their husbands attend the mosque. Lessons are given at the mosque so that Arabic can be learnt and the Qur'an may be read in its original language.

Judaism

In Judaism, families observe Shabbat (the Sabbath). This includes spending time together, hearing stories from the Torah and resting. At festivals historical events are remembered, such as remembering God sparing the Jews in Egypt at Pesach. Children ask their parents about why the festival is celebrated and to explain the significance of the food on the Seder plate. At the age of five children are sent to classes to learn Hebrew and Jewish religious history and principles.

C *Pesach Seder plate*

Sikhism

In Sikhism parents teach their children the importance of the name of God and they learn the first hymn of the Adi Granth. Children are introduced to worship and the gurdwara.

Discussion activity 👥

With a partner, in a small group or as a class, discuss what you think are the most important influences on a person's behaviour, decision-making and life choices. Contrast possible differences between influences on people in religious and non-religious homes. Make notes to draw on when revising for your examination.

Activities

1 Explain the importance of the home and upbringing in guiding a child to make right decisions.

2 'All young people should receive an understanding of religion in their homes.' What do you think? Explain your opinion.

AQA *Examiner's tip*

Be aware of how children are brought up to understand their religion and its traditions and be able to give specific examples for the religions you are studying.

Summary

You should now be able to explain the importance of the home and upbringing in influencing young people in their decision-making and understand the relevance of religion.

6.3   Moral codes

■ 'Golden rule'

The 'golden rule' of treating other people as you wish to be treated is common to all the major religions, along with the understanding that decisions, actions and failures to act have consequences. Young people in religious families learn the importance of these ideas. They form part of the **moral codes** that the young people are taught to follow.

Religion	Teaching	Source
Buddhism	'Just as a mother would protect her only child with her life, even so let one cultivate a boundless love towards all beings.'	Khuddaka Patha, from the Metta Sutta
Christianity	'Love your neighbour as yourself.'	Mark 12:31
Hinduism	'This is the sum of duty: do nought to others which if done to thee would cause thee pain.'	The Mahabharata
Islam	'No one of you is a believer until he desires for his brother that which he desires for himself.'	Hadith
Judaism	'Love your neighbour as yourself.'	Leviticus 19:18
Sikhism	'I am a stranger to no one and no one is a stranger to me. Indeed, I am a friend to all.'	Guru Granth Sahib

A   *The 'golden rule' in the major religions*

Objectives

Know about and be able to explain the importance of the moral codes of the religions being studied in a young believer's life.

Key terms

Moral codes: moral rules by which a person decides to live.

AQA   *Examiner's tip*

If you use a quotation in the examination, it is a good idea to say whom you are quoting, although it is not essential.

■ Moral codes

Young people need to have something to draw on when making decisions about behaviour. This is made up of the experience they have gained of the world; their conscience (their inner feeling that they are doing right or wrong); and, for religious people, the moral codes taught by their religion, examined below.

Buddhism

Moral codes, which are rules to live by, are often believed to come from a deity, but this is not the case in Buddhism. The Eightfold Path, for example, is the teaching of the Buddha. It is believed to be the way to end suffering and reach enlightenment and Nibbana. It involves having the right (meaning correct or best possible) understanding, intention, speech, action, occupation, effort, mindfulness and concentration. The first two steps on the Path are about wisdom, the next three are about morality and the final three are about mental development.

Christianity

In Christianity, the moral codes include the Ten Commandments (Exodus 20:3–17) and the Sermon on the Mount (Matthew 5–7). Together with the golden rule (Mark 12:31) these teachings form the basis of Christian morality. Young Christians are brought up to not be selfish in their attitudes.

B   *A Japanese statue of Buddha*

Hinduism

In Hinduism, children are traditionally taught the 10 *yamas*: that they should act in a non-violent manner (ahimsa), speak the truth, not steal, be faithful in marriage, have patience, have perseverance, have compassion, be honest, have a moderate appetite and avoid anything that is impure. Hindus have 10 traditional niyamas (observances). This means that they are expected to show sorrow for doing wrong, be content, give without thought of reward, have faith in religious teachings, worship through prayer and meditation, study the scriptures, follow guidance from the gurus, fulfil religious vows, chant mantras and endure extremes (such as heat and cold).

Judaism

The formation of moral codes in Jewish young people comes from a developing knowledge of the Torah, including the Ten Commandments and the 613 mitzvot (commandments). For example, kashrut laws (food laws) are likely to affect what a Jew will eat or not eat, which will affect a person's lifestyle.

C   *The Torah Scrolls containing the Ten Commandments*

Islam

Islam has well defined value systems, which children are taught. These are based on the Qur'an and the Hadith (sayings of Muhammad). Muslim children are made aware of the importance of modesty, faithfulness in marriage, and things that are forbidden because of the harm they bring, such as drinking alcohol and gambling. These moral codes affect the life choices Muslims make.

Sikhism

Sikh children are taught the Rahit Maryada (Sikh code of discipline). This includes not cutting their hair, not using tobacco or other intoxicants such as alcohol, not eating meat that has been ritually slaughtered (such as halal meat) and not committing adultery.

AQA   Examiner's tip

Learn a quotation about the golden rule for the religions you are studying as you will probably be able to use it in answering at least one question in the exam. Referring to sacred texts will help to gain marks.

Research activity

Use the internet or a library to find out more about the moral codes for the religions you are studying and record your findings to draw on when preparing for the examination.

Discussion activity

With a partner, in a small group or as a class, discuss the value of moral codes in modern society. Give reasons for your opinion. Make notes on the opinions given and the reasons for them.

Summary

You should now be able to discuss the moral codes for the religion(s) you are studying and explain their importance in a young believers' life.

Activities

1   Explain what is meant by the golden rule and include a quotation from the scriptures for the religion(s) you are studying.

2   Outline details of the moral codes for the religion(s) you are studying.

3   'There should be one moral code of conduct for everyone, young or old, religious or not.' What do you think? Explain your opinion.

Religious organisations for young people

Members of different faiths have founded many youth clubs and youth organisations. These clubs, provide opportunities for young people to:

- learn about their faith and have a pride in their religion
- be helped in forming their moral codes
- learn how to become useful citizens
- take part in fun and adventurous activities
- win awards and badges
- learn new skills
- build relationships with like-minded young people of the same faith.

Brigades

Some youth clubs are known as a **brigade**, and are studied in the case study boxes below.

Case study

Boys' Brigade

One of the oldest of the youth organisations is the Boys' Brigade (BB), founded by Sir William Alexander Smith in Glasgow in 1883. A Christian organisation, it provided a semi-military style discipline with marching, education, fun activities including gymnastics and summer camps. These ideas brought immediate success. Soon other companies (groups of BB members) started and during the 1890s the BB became an international organisation. Robert Baden-Powell, founder of the Scouts movement, was a Vice President of the Boys' Brigade.

Today in the UK and Republic of Ireland there are over 1,500 BB companies. Wearing the BB uniform, around 60,000 young people aged 5–18 take part in weekly activities that lead to badges for various achievements. Members learn new skills and compete in various competitions as well as learn about the Christian faith. The BB is famous for its bugle bands.

The BB still uses the original objective 'The advancement of Christ's kingdom among boys and the promotion of habits of obedience, reverence, discipline, self-respect and all that tends towards a true Christian manliness needs.'

B *The motto of the Boys' Brigade is 'Sure and steadfast', which is based on Hebrews 6:19*

∞ links

Find out more at:

www.boys-brigade.org.uk

Girls' Brigade

Another Christian youth organisation is the Girls' Brigade (GB). The GB started in 1893 at Sandymount Presbyterian Church in Dublin, Ireland and today has companies in over 60 countries. In the UK, around 30,000 young people aged 4–18 take part in many different activities and work towards achieving badges in four themes: spiritual, physical, educational and service. The aim of the GB is 'To help girls become followers of the Lord Jesus Christ, and through self-control, reverence and a sense of responsibility to find true enrichment of life'. The motto is to 'Seek, serve and follow Christ.'

In the 1960s, three Christian youth groups joined together to form the modern GB. The cross in the centre came from the Girls' Brigade and symbolises Jesus' sacrifice. The lamp came from The Girls' Guildry and shows the light of the Girls' Brigade shining upon the world. The crown came from the Girls' Life Brigade and represents Christ as King. The torch represents the flame of Christ's living spirit.

C   *The Girls' Brigade crest*

Research activity

2   Use the Girls' Brigade website (see Links) to discover more about the GB sections, badge work, projects and principles. Record some of their activities, including examples of what is done to obtain the spiritual badges.

links

Find out more at:

www.girlsbrigadeew.org.uk

The Jewish Lads' and Girls' Brigade (JLGB)

In 1895, Colonel Albert E. W. Goldsmid formed the Jewish Lads' Brigade in London. Its aim was set out as 'to instil into the rising generation from their earliest years habits of orderliness, cleanliness, and honour, so that in learning to respect themselves they will do credit to their community.' In many ways this was the Jewish equivalent of the Boys' Brigade, but the organisation concentrated less on religious teaching and more on moral behaviour and social action.

The earliest Jewish youth clubs in Britain were set up for girls. From them developed the Jewish Girls' Brigade until the amalgamation with the Jewish Lads Brigade in 1974 and the formation of the JLGB. There are nearly 4,000 members of the JLGB in Britain.

links

Find out more at:

www.jlgb.org

Research activity

3   Use the Jewish Lads' and Girls' Brigade website (see Links) to discover more about the purpose of the JLGB. Record what sections there are and what religious and non-religious activities are included in their programme.

Discussion activity

In pairs, groups, or as a class, discuss the advantages and disadvantages for young people of belonging to religious organisations like the brigades. Make notes on the opinions given and the reasons for them.

Summary

You should now be able to explain why religions have youth groups and have considered the work of young groups such as the brigades.

Events for young people

Members of many of the different faiths run special events for young people, such as camps where they may stay and join in various activities. Some are international, others are mainly for adventure activities, while some are designed to teach those who attend more about their faith.

- Most Buddhist camps combine social and physical activities with learning about meditation and other spiritual practices.
- The Elms International Camp held near Oxford for 11–19 year olds has grown to become Europe's leading Jewish summer camp. Young Jews from around the world meet to make friends and learn about their faith.
- Christian events for young people include **Spring Harvest** and **Taizé**. These are covered in more detail in the case studies below.

Abseiling, archery, beach volleyball, canoeing, climbing, fencing, football, kayaking, Laser Quest and quad biking are typical activities at these adventure holidays. Some religious events or places have become so well known that young people in their thousands and sometimes from many parts of the world are attracted to attend.

Research activity

1. Use the internet or library to find out more about the youth camps organised by the religions you are studying, such as Dharma Drum for Young People, Lake Bloomington Hindu Camp, Muslim Student Camp and Sikh Student Camp.

2. What religious magazines are published for young people for the religions you are studying? Record what activities and events they advertise.

A Sometimes stadiums are hired for large events of worship, as at this Christian event

Case study

Spring Harvest

Since its launch in Prestatyn, Wales, in 1979, Spring Harvest has grown to become the largest Christian conference in Europe. The annual main event occurs for three weeks each Easter at two Butlins holiday camps. There is a combined attendance of around 50,000 people of all ages. There is an emphasis on modern worship music, workshops and Bible study groups, with programmes for different age groups and big top meetings in the evenings. Its aim is to equip Christians, including young people, for action in their local community and the organisation also runs other conferences, courses and events throughout the year. Spring Harvest has also a range of resources for young people including Bible study aids, songbooks and Christian lifestyle books.

Taizé

The Taizé community was founded by Brother Roger in Burgundy, France, in 1940, to focus on prayer and Christian meditation. Over 100 Protestant and Catholic brothers from around 30 different countries live in the community. Each week thousands of young people aged 15 and over come from all over the world to join in the community life. Prayers are held three times a day. Songs, including chants that can be learnt quickly, have been developed and Taizé music is used in churches across the world. Each morning, brothers of the community introduce a Bible passage. This is followed by a time of silent reflection and sharing in small groups. In the afternoon, many attend song practice before going to international workshops on issues such as world peace or doing practical work to help the community. After supper, there is evening prayer with songs in the church. Some decide to spend the week or the weekend in silence, making time to try to listen to God.

B   *Teenagers discuss a Bible passage, a typical activity at Taizé*

Young people and worship

There are also special worship activities provided for young people in most religions. Here are some examples from Christianity:

- Some Sunday services have 'all-age worship', which may include drama, action songs, quizzes, dancing and stories appropriate for people of all ages.
- Other churches have Junior Church (Sunday school), which follows a separate programme from the adults' worship.
- Christian organisations like Scripture Union provide suitable materials for different age groups.
- It has been the tradition in some denominations (like Methodists) to have an annual Junior Church Anniversary. Here the young people present a programme of Christian songs, drama, readings and recitations.
- Other churches may have activities, such as Sunday Club, which includes games and teaching, or Café Church, where food is shared together.

'Some would describe Spring Harvest as an action-packed week at a holiday camp, whereas Taizé is a place of quiet reflection.' With a partner, in a small group or as a class discuss this description. What else might be said about what happens at Spring Harvest and Taizé?

1 Give two reasons why religious camps have become popular.

2 Explain why Spring Harvest might be important to some Christians.

3 'Times of quiet reflection are becoming more important in a busy world.' What do you think? Explain your opinion.

Be prepared to use at least one case study to answer questions about activities of faith groups for young people.

You should now understand special events that are organised for young people by the different religions and be able to explain why religious groups have special worship for young people.

Celebrations and festivals

Each religion has many joyful occasions, including celebrations at the birth of a new child, commitment ceremonies and festivals remembering key events in the history of the faith. Young people are able to learn about their religion while having an enjoyable time.

Objectives

Investigate some key celebrations and festivals that involve young people.

Buddhism

Many Buddhist celebrations are centred on the life and teachings of the Buddha. Wesak celebrates the Buddha's birth, enlightenment and death. Lights and decorations are put up in the home for this colourful festival. In Thailand, children help to make lanterns out of paper and wood and cards are sent to friends. One Wesak ceremony includes the release of caged birds. Chinese Buddhists include dancing dragons as part of their celebrations and gifts are given to charity. In Sri Lanka, young people celebrate the festival of Poson by letting off firecrackers. This festival reminds them of the arrival of Emperor Ashoka's son Mahinda in their country. Songkran, the Buddhist New Year, is also an important festival.

A *Colourful decorations are put up for Wesak*

Christianity

The Christian festivals of Christmas and Easter are particularly enjoyed by young people. The celebration of the birth of Jesus at Christmas includes giving presents, sending cards, singing carols, performing nativity plays, parties, eating special foods, and decorating homes and public spaces. At Easter, chocolate eggs are given. The eggs symbolise new life and celebrate Jesus's resurrection.

Hinduism

Diwali is a favourite of young people. This Festival of Light includes firecrackers, fireworks, giving and receiving presents and eating sweets, such as laddoo and barfi. The festival symbolises the victory of good over evil. Lights or lamps are lit in the home and sometimes floated down rivers. A fun festival in spring is Holi, the Festival of Colours, which celebrates new life and the triumph of good over evil.

B *Diwali lamps in India*

It is dedicated to Krishna. A bonfire is built and an effigy of the demoness Holika is burned on it. Children and adults throw coloured powder or paint and water at each other. There is dancing and singing and children are carried around the fire. Gifts of sweets and flowers are often given.

Islam

Young people under the age of 12 are gradually introduced to fasting during the month of Ramadan. They build up to the full fast during daylight hours by going without a little more food and drink each year. The festival of Eid-ul-Fitr breaks this month of discipline and spiritual devotion. Friends and relatives gather together, meeting in homes and in the mosque for special prayers. Their best or new clothes are worn. There are parties, particularly for young people, presents are given and Eid cards are sent.

Judaism

A festival that Jewish young people particularly enjoy is that of Purim. This commemorates the victory of Queen Esther over the wicked Haman. There is a lot of eating and drinking at the festival and gifts are exchanged. The main celebration is the reading of the Book of Esther. Whenever the name Haman is mentioned everyone tries to drown it out with rattles or by stamping, booing and hissing. Students perform a play in which they mock their teachers. At the festival called Pesach, young people are involved in a conversation recalling the events of the angel of death passing over Egypt.

Sikhism

Diwali is celebrated in similar style to Hindus and the Golden Temple at Amritsar is lit up by hundreds of lights. Another important Sikh festival is Baisakhi. It celebrates the Sikh New Year and the anniversary of the 1699 founding of the Khalsa by Guru Gobind Singh. Sikhs regard this event as the start of the Sikh community. Its anniversary is a day for rejoicing for people of all ages, and for initiating new members into the Khalsa. A service in the gurdwara reminds everyone of the historical events and the cloth around the flagpole and the Nishan Sahib (flag) is renewed.

Discussion activity 👥

With a partner, in a small group or as a class, discuss the value of celebrating festivals. Do you think that young people in Britain should be encouraged to celebrate the festivals of all the major religions?

Activities

1. Describe how young people are involved in celebrating festivals in the religions you are studying.

2. Explain why these festivals are important for young people.

3. 'All religious festivals should have particular activities for young people.' What do you think? Explain your opinion.

Summary

You should now be able to explain how young people are involved in festival celebrations in the religions you are studying.

AQA *Examiner's tip*

Focus in particular on the activities enjoyed by young people in the religions you are studying and be prepared to evaluate the value of these festivals for them.

C *Hamentachen pastry eaten at Purim*

D *Hannukah and Christmas being celebrated together*

■ Ceremonies for young people

Most religions have ceremonies for young people approaching adulthood. Some ceremonies enable a believer to show commitment to their faith (a promise of agreement), while others celebrate a young person becoming recognised as an adult. During these ceremonies the individual takes on the rights, rules and responsibilities associated with their religion. These are known as coming-of-age ceremonies.

Buddhism

In Buddhism there no coming-of-age ceremony, but when a Buddhist young man regards himself as mature enough he may show commitment by becoming ordained. Most are about 20 when they go through this process. In preparation for the ceremony they have their head shaved, dress in white, and are given a new monastic name, all signifying the beginning of a new life. If questions about his genuineness are answered satisfactorily the young man will be allowed entry into the sangha and will wear the robe of a monk. He is given a spiritual master and begins his spiritual training. A young woman may wish to follow the same route to become a nun.

A   *Their shaved heads and robes show that these young Buddhist men and women have been ordained*

Christianity

In some Christian denominations, membership or **confirmation** classes are held for those who wish to confirm the promises made on their behalf at their infant baptism (christening). Those attending are taught about the faith and their responsibilities as Christians.

Confirmation

Confirmation is a popular practice in the Roman Catholic and Anglican churches. It enables the participant to be regarded as a full member of the Christian community. In the Catholic Church, confirmation can happen from the age of seven and after this the young people can take their first communion and share in the bread and wine of the Mass. In practice, even in the Catholic Church, Christian confirmation or membership ceremonies usually take place at a later date, when a person is in their teens. Many think this ensures that the individual is old enough to be aware of what they are doing and gives them the freedom to choose whether or not confirmation is for them. In Anglican and Roman Catholic churches, a bishop usually conducts the ceremony and Christians believe that they receive the gift of the Holy Spirit. In the Anglican Church the bishop lays his hands on the head of the person being confirmed and prays for them to receive the gift. In the Roman Catholic Church, each participant is also anointed with oil. Many Protestant churches, such as the Methodists, receive people as members of their denomination rather than performing confirmation ceremonies.

B   Roman Catholic confirmation ceremony

Hinduism

In Hinduism, when a boy shaves for the first time it indicates that he has come of age. This is celebrated with the Kesanta Samskara ceremony, which includes giving gifts and throwing the shaved hair into water. Often a vow of celibacy is taken. When girls reach puberty they take part in the ritual kala ceremony at home. Only women are present to give the girl her first sari, sing songs of praise and give her gifts such as jewellery and new clothing. Both these ceremonies signify that the young person is mature enough to understand their responsibility towards family, religion and society. Some Hindus take part in a sacred thread ceremony for boys to mark their coming of age. After this they are considered old enough to do religious ceremonies. The ceremony of Samavartana marks the end of the stage of being a student. The young person then decides either to adopt the family life path or that of monastic life.

C   Hindu girls receive their first sari when they reach puberty

Activities

1   Explain what happens at the ceremonies of commitment or coming of age for the religions you are studying.

2   'There is no need for coming of age ceremonies.' What do you think? Explain your opinion.

Discussion activity

With a partner, in a small group or as a class, discuss the following statement. What do you think? Try to consider a range of points of view, and make notes on key points that you can use when revising for the examination.

'Coming of age ceremonies are more for the parents to realise that their children have grown up than for the individual to understand the rights and responsibilities that they have now undertaken.'

AQA Examiner's tip

If there are differences in how these ceremonies are celebrated within a religious tradition, it is an advantage to be able to explain these differences.

Summary

You should now be able to explain the ceremonies associated with coming of age and/or commitment for Buddhism, Christianity or Hinduism.

Islam

There is no particular coming-of-age of ceremony in Islam, but before puberty a child does not have to carry out the obligatory acts of Shari'ah. Gradually, young people are introduced to the responsibilities of being a Muslim. For example, it is recommended but not compulsory for a child to pray at the age of seven. At puberty, praying becomes a duty, along with other obligations, such as fasting during Ramadan. Young people are then made aware of Muslim rules about relationships, for example that sex outside of marriage is forbidden.

Objectives

Investigate rights and responsibilities and coming-of-age ceremonies in Islam, Judaism and Sikhism.

links

For similar ceremonies in Buddhism, Christianity and Hinduism, see pages 130–131.

A At puberty, prayer becomes a duty for young Muslims

Judaism

The coming-of-age ceremonies in Judaism, **Bar Mitzvah** and **Bat Mitzvah**, are described in the case study boxes below.

Key terms

Bar Mitzvah: 'Son of Commandment' – initiation ceremony for 13-year-old boys.

Bat Mitzvah: 'Daughter of Commandment' – initiation ceremony for 12-year-old girls.

Case study

Bar Mitzvah

The Bar Mitzvah celebrations take place when a Jewish boy reaches the age of 13. This ceremony signifies that the boy is old enough to be responsible for his own actions. He is given the full rights and privileges of being a Jewish adult and also takes on the responsibilities. The rights include being able to wear the tallit (prayer shawl) and the tefillin (leather boxes containing biblical texts) and read from the Torah in the synagogue. He becomes part of the minyan (10 men needed for a service) and the Bar Mitzvah ceremony allows him to show his commitment to Judaism. He becomes a 'son of the commandment'. Before this, his parents were responsible for him following Jewish laws and traditions and keeping the Ten Commandments. The ceremony includes reading from the Sefer Torah in Hebrew, and his father blessing him and thanking God that his son is now responsible for his own actions. A meal is eaten at which the young man thanks everyone for their gifts, thanks his parents for what they have done for him, and sets out his religious hopes for the future.

B Reading the Torah at a Bar Mitzvah ceremony

Bat Mitzvah

The ceremony for Jewish girls is called the Bat Mitzvah. Their coming of age is 12 and Bat Mitzvah means 'Daughter of the Commandment'. Like the boys, they are now regarded as responsible for their own decisions and are expected to keep the Jewish laws and traditions. The ceremony takes place on the Shabbat and girls may read from the Talmud. It is a time of celebration and the receiving of gifts. Many Orthodox Jews do not take part in Bat Mitzvah ceremonies.

Sikhism

In Sikhism, an initiation ceremony called the Dastaar Bandi takes place when a person is aged between 14 and 16. This celebrates the wearing of the boy's first turban. The Amrit Samskar ceremony initiates baptised teenaged Sikhs into the Khalsa and they wear the five Ks. It takes place in front of the Guru Granth Sahib and five members of the Khalsa. The Sikh faith is explained and the initiate is asked to accept the Sikh principles for living. Special prayers for God's protection are said. Amrit (a special solution of sugar and water) is prepared in an iron bowl. This is blessed and sprinkled on the hair, eyes and ears of the person joining the Khalsa. They repeat the Mool Mantar (statement of belief) five times. They are then received as either a son or daughter of Guru Gobind Singh and have taken on the rights and responsibilities of being a Khalsa Sikh. This means that they are expected to follow the Rahit Maryada (rules of conduct). These teach, for example, that sexual relationships should be within marriage and forbid adultery. Boys are given the name Singh (lion) and girls Kaur (princess). Everyone present then shares Prashad (holy food made from ground wheat, sugar and ghee, or clarified butter).

Extension activity

Use the internet or library to find out more about the coming-of-age ceremonies for the religion(s) you are studying. Make notes on your findings to use when preparing for the examination.

Discussion activity

Some say that the real value of coming-of-age ceremonies is that when puberty arrives they make the individual aware of rules concerning relationships with the opposite sex. With a partner, in a small group or as a class, discuss what you think are the most important reasons for such ceremonies.

AQA   Examiner's tip

Be able to discuss and explain what it means to become an adult under the rules and regulations of a religion.

Activities

1   Explain what happens at the coming-of-age ceremony for the religions you are studying.

2   Give examples of the rights, rules and responsibilities those undertaking coming-of-age ceremonies agree to follow.

3   'Everyone should have the freedom of choice concerning whether or not they want a coming-of-age ceremony.' What do you think? Explain your opinion.

Summary

You should now be able to explain the importance of coming-of-age ceremonies in Islam, Judaism and Sikhism and consider the rights and responsibilities associated with adulthood.

Problems and benefits associated with belief

Issues for religious young people

There are a number of issues that may affect the wellbeing, beliefs and behaviour of religious young people in Britain today.

Generation gap

Generation gap is the term often used to describe the differences between the views of young people and their parents and elders, when they do not understand each other because of their different experiences, beliefs, opinions, habits and behaviour. Different tastes in music and fashion, ideas about the importance of religion, and attitudes towards culture, drugs, sex, the digital revolution, politics and behaviour can all make relationships between age groups difficult. Prejudices may prevent sensible dialogue and cause misunderstandings. For example, 'hoodies are vandals', or 'old people haven't got a clue'.

Marginalisation

Those who do not fit in with the behaviour expected for an age group such as teenagers may become marginalised. **Marginalisation** may involve being teased or left out. For example, a young person may find it difficult if all their friends join a Sunday football club, but they instead attend religious classes and take part in worship. The young person could be marginalised from that group of friends. However, he or she is likely to find a group of friends who also take religion seriously.

Peer pressure

Peer pressure is influence exerted by friends or others of the same age to change a person's attitudes, values or behaviour to be the same as the group. The person who receives this pressure may not wish to do what the others are doing, such as having sex outside of marriage, smoking cigarettes or taking drugs. Peer pressure is not always negative, however. A young person in a group that works hard, is active in sport or achieves academically may feel they have to do the same. In the end, the group pressure may help them improve their lives.

Religious belief in a secular society

Increasingly Britain has become a **secular** society, with fewer religious people. In the past, most people went to church on Sundays. Now Sunday is like a normal weekday, with many people shopping or taking part in leisure activities. For most British people, religion is not at the centre of their lives, but there is a tolerance of those who wish to believe. A secular society does not necessarily insist on everyone behaving and thinking the same, but expects people to keep within the secular law. Young people may have the freedom of choice to accept or reject religious belief.

Objectives

Understand the problems and benefits associated with belief and young people.

Key terms

Generation gap: a difference between the views of young people and their parents.

Marginalisation: the social process of becoming or being isolated and left out.

Peer pressure: influence exerted by friends on each other.

Secular: not religious.

⚭ links

For the definition of prejudice and more on prejudice based on age, see pages 52–53 and 56–57.

A 'You don't understand, Dad!'

Empowerment and purpose

The different faiths in Britain have provided **empowerment** opportunities for young people to learn and participate in activities and events for their age groups. Those who wish to be involved in religion are encouraged to do so. It is through such a wish that many find **purpose** in life and an explanation of why we are here. For example, Buddhists may say that their purpose is to help all living beings to end their suffering, whereas a Muslim might argue that life is a test and a preparation for the world to come. So spirituality leads many people to believe that they understand some of the mysteries of life and to have an aim in life.

Brotherhood

Belonging to a faith enables people to feel a part of something much larger than themselves. In Islam it is called the ummah, or **brotherhood**. Members of a major faith are part of the worldwide religion. Wherever believers go, they are likely to meet 'brothers and sisters' in the faith. There is an immediate bond between them as they share similar beliefs and religious practices.

⚭ links

See pages 124–127 for more about religious activities and events for young people.

B   *Young people may find a group of friends through their religion*

Key terms

Empowerment: an individual having the right to make their own choices and act on them.

Purpose: the goal of life and the reason for living.

Brotherhood: people of similar beliefs regard themselves like brothers.

C   *Sisters in faith*

Discussion activity 👤👤👤

With a partner, in a small group or as a class, discuss whether or not you believe that there is pressure on young people to reject the idea of religion in Britain today. Give reasons for your opinion and make notes to prepare you for your examination.

Activities

1   Explain what is meant by the generation gap, marginalisation, peer pressure and secular society.

2   Explain the positive benefits a young person might feel are associated with religious belief.

3   'Religion helps a young person find a real purpose to life.' What do you think? Explain your opinion.

AQA Examiner's tip

Be able to explain and evaluate the problems young people face and the benefits they may gain in British society if they are members of a religious faith.

Summary

You should now be able to explain the problems and benefits associated with belief and young people.

▇ Religious Education in schools

The state has long regarded Religious Studies (Religious Education) as an important subject for all students and so has introduced laws to ensure that it is taught in British schools. The Education Reform Act of 1988, confirmed by the Education Acts of 1996 and 1998, sets out the legal requirements for Religious Education (RE), summarised below.

- RE must be provided for all students in state schools from reception classes to sixth forms.

- Unlike other subjects, local education authorities provide a locally agreed syllabus, including input from the local faith groups. This means that RE should include Christianity and the other major religions, such as Buddhism, Hinduism, Islam, Judaism and Sikhism. The syllabus must:

> 66   *...reflect the fact that the religious traditions in Great Britain are in the main Christian, while taking account of the teachings and practices of the other principal religions represented in Great Britain.* 99
>
> *ERA, 1988 Section 8 (3)*

- Independent schools must provide RE in accordance with the Trust Deed of the school and wishes of the governors.

- Sixth-form colleges must provide RE for students who request it.

- Special schools do not have to follow the locally agreed syllabus, but are expected to include RE in their curriculum.

Aims and responsibilities of RE

RE lessons should not be used to persuade students to join a particular religion. Rather, the aims of RE are to promote the spiritual, moral, social and cultural development of young people. This enables the subject to embrace the beliefs, teachings and practices of the different faiths and to debate moral issues affecting society. Schools develop young people in the ways described through many subject areas, and not just through RE. Schools have the responsibility of preparing young people for adulthood and life in society. Education in British traditions, religions and culture is an important part of this.

Objectives

Investigate the role of schools in the religious education of young people.

 RE is for students of all ages

Assemblies

According to the School Standards and Framework Act 1998, state schools should provide **assemblies** (collective worship) each day. Assemblies may be led by teachers, often members of the school senior management team. They may involve a talk, such as a reflection on a moral or spiritual theme, singing and prayers. Sometimes guest speakers, such as leaders of local faith groups, are invited to participate or students may contribute through drama or music. Themes in the assemblies are not always religious. They may be about issues, such as working together to improve the environment or making the most of the opportunities the school offers. Collective worship gives an opportunity for spiritual and moral education, but its purpose is not to try to persuade young people to join a particular faith.

Faith schools

There are currently over 7,000 **faith schools** in the UK. Most are Church of England. These are mainly Roman Catholic, Methodists and other denominational schools. Britain also has more than 30 Jewish schools, some Muslim schools, one Hindu and one Sikh school. All faith schools are all encouraged to teach about faiths other than their own. Some people involved in education are concerned that faith schools may divide the community rather than encouraging multiculturalism and tolerance. Others believe that faith schools give young people a greater opportunity to learn more about their religion and traditions than normal state schools.

> **Key terms**
>
> **Assemblies**: occasions when students get together for 'collective worship'.
>
> **Faith schools**: schools run by a particular religion rather than by the state.

A Hindu school

Case study

The first state-funded Hindu school is the Krishna Avanti Voluntary Aided Primary School in Edgware, North London. This is an area where almost a third of people are Hindu and the school's education is based on Hindu values and beliefs. Students follow the National Curriculum but have the opportunity to take part in Hindu practices such as meditation and yoga. All school meals are vegetarian and students are taught the classical Sanskrit language.

> **Discussion activity**
>
> With a partner, in a small group or as a class, discuss the advantages and disadvantages of faith schools. Try to consider different points of view, and make notes of key points raised that you can refer to in your revision.

> **AQA   Examiner's tip**
>
> You need to know the law regarding RE and assemblies in order to know the background to the aims of RE and collective worship.

> **Activities**
>
> 1   Describe the role of schools in providing students with RS lessons.
>
> 2   Explain why this is regarded as important.
>
> 3   'All assemblies should have a spiritual focus.' What do you think? Explain your opinion.

> **Summary**
>
> You should now be able to explain the role of schools (including faith schools) in providing RE and assemblies for young people.

6

Religion and young people – summary

For the examination you should now be able to:

✔ describe birth and initiation ceremonies

✔ explain the importance of the home, upbringing, moral codes and spirituality and their role in decision-making and life choices

✔ explain the activities of faith groups for young people including festivals and special events

✔ describe and explain the ceremonies that are used to show commitment to a faith and the coming of age

✔ explain the rights and responsibilities that go with membership of a religion

✔ evaluate the problems and benefits for young people associated with belief

✔ explain the role of schools in enabling young people to learn more about religious belief.

Sample answer

1 Write an answer to the following exam question.

'Religion is not relevant to young people.'

Do you agree? Give reasons for your answer, showing that you have thought about more than one point of view. Refer to religious arguments in your answer.

(6 marks)

2 Read the following sample answer.

In Britain it is mostly older people who attend church or who worship God and services are geared to an older generation. Young children may be taken to Junior Church or the place of worship for their religion by their parents but most teenagers decide that religion is not for them. Most young people find worship uninteresting and would rather do something else. Listening to someone preach about something they do not understand is not their favourite pastime. Listening to pop music, playing a computer game, partying or chatting to friends is much more appealing.

Some young people do find religion relevant and enjoy activities like going to Spring Harvest or Taizé. There are special activities organised for young people of different ages, which makes religion relevant to them. Traditional methods of worship may not seem particularly interesting, but now new methods using modern technology are being introduced.

The major problem is peer pressure from those who do not believe in God. I think that religion is relevant to some young people, but others have either turned their back on it or have not been prepared to give religion a try in the first place.

3 With a partner, discuss the sample answer. Do you think that there are other things that the student could have included in the answer?

4 What mark would you give this answer out of six? What are the reasons for the mark you have given? Look at the mark scheme in the Introduction on page 7 (AO2) to help you make a decision.

AQA Examination-style questions

1   Look at the photograph and answer the following questions.

(a) Give an example of a religious moral code.   *(1 mark)*

If the command word is 'Give', you do not have to offer an explanation.
An answer like 'The Ten Commandments' would be sufficient.

(b) Explain what happens at one membership or coming-of-age ceremony.   *(4 marks)*

If the trigger word is 'explain', include the importance and/or symbolism of the actions.

(c) 'The best way for young people to learn about religion is through Religious Studies lessons.' What do you think? Explain your opinion.   *(3 marks)*

This question is not asking for a balanced response so you do not need to give both sides of the argument.

(d) Explain the benefits for young people of belonging to a religion.   *(4 marks)*

Notice that 'benefits' is plural so do not confine your answer to one idea as you will limit yourself to a maximum of two marks.

(e) 'Religions should provide more activities for young people.' Do you agree? Give reasons for your answer, showing that you have thought about more than one point of view.   *(6 marks)*

When asked if you agree with a statement, explain what you think, and why others might disagree. One-sided answers can only achieve four marks. Include religious arguments; without this you can achive only three marks.

Glossary

A

Abortion: the deliberate termination (ending) of a pregnancy, usually before the foetus is 24 weeks old and viable.

Abortion Act (1967): the first law making abortion legal in England, Scotland and Wales.

Abuse: misuse of the world and the environment.

Acid rain: rain made acid by contamination through pollution in the atmosphere as the result of emissions from factories, vehicles, power stations, and so on.

Adoption: the legal process where a person (child) is taken (adopted) into the family as a son or daughter.

Ageism: prejudice against someone because of their age, leading to discrimination.

Animal experiments: testing on animals, either for medical or cosmetic purposes, to ensure the product is safe for use by humans.

Animal exports: the selling of animals to other countries.

Animal rights: the belief that animals have a dignity just as humans do and should be given care and protection.

Assemblies: occasions when students get together for 'collective worship'.

Assisi Declarations: statements about the need to protect animals and the environment made on behalf of the different major religions.

Awe: a feeling of respect; insight into meaning greater than oneself.

B

Backbone: spinal column.

Bar Mitzvah: 'Son of Commandment' – initiation ceremony for 13-year-old boys.

Bat Mitzvah: 'Daughter of Commandment' – initiation ceremony for 12-year-old girls.

Big bang: scientific theory that the universe began with an enormous explosion.

Biodegradable: able to be broken down by bacteria in the environment.

Biological weapons: weapons that have living organisms or infective material that can lead to disease or death.

Birth: passing down the birth canal and living outside the mother.

Blessing: the idea that God has favoured a couple with a child.

Brigade: a uniformed religious youth organisation for young people.

Brotherhood: people of similar beliefs regard themselves like brothers.

Bull fighting: associated in particular with Spain, matadors fight bulls (and eventually kill them) to entertain the crowds.

C

Carbon emissions: release of greenhouse gases, such as carbon monoxide from vehicles, into the atmosphere.

Chemical weapons: weapons that use chemicals to poison, burn, paralyse humans and the natural environment.

Chlorofluorocarbons (CFCs): chemicals in refrigerators, aerosols and air conditioners that destroy the ozone layer.

Class: social group or caste, position in society.

Climate change: the idea that the climate is getting warmer (global warming).

Cloning: the scientific method by which animals or plants can be created which have exactly the same genetic make-up as the original, because the DNA of the original is used.

Colour: skin colour, usually non-white.

Coming of age: a young person's transition from adolescence to adulthood.

Commitment: a pledge, promise or affirmation of agreement.

Compassion: a feeling of pity that makes one want to help.

Conception: when sperm meets egg.

Confirmation: a sacrament admitting a baptised person to full participation in the church.

Conflict: fighting, a state of discord or war.

Conscience: the inner feeling that you are doing right or wrong.

Conscientious objectors: people who object to fighting in a war because killing is against their conscience.

Conservation: looking after the environment and protecting animals.

Conventional weapons: weapons that do not contain biological, chemical or nuclear elements.

Creation: belief that God created the universe and everything in it.

D

Deforestation: the cutting down of large amounts of forest, usually because of business needs.

Design: the argument that God designed (made) the universe because everything is so intricately made in its detail that it could not have happened by chance.

Destruction of crops: food crops destroyed by weather conditions.

Deterrent: a way of discouraging enemy attack by being able to retaliate.

Disability: physical or mental handicap or impairment.

Disarmament: getting rid of weapons.

Discrimination: actions as a result of prejudice.

DNA: deoxyribonucleic acid that carries genetic information in a cell.

Droughts: long periods of abnormally low rainfall.

E

Earth Summits: informal name for United Nations Conferences on Environment and Development.

Embryo: fertilised ovum at about 12-14 days when implanted into the wall of the womb.

Emissions: a substance discharged into the air.

Empowerment: an individual having the right to make their own choices and act on them.

Ensouled: receives a soul.

Equality: that people should be given the same rights and opportunities regardless of sex, religion, race, etc.

Evolution (evolved): theory that says living things change gradually over a long time.

Experience: something that happens to a person.

Extinction: when all members of a species have died out and that species will never exist on Earth again.

F

Factory farming: when animals are used for meat or dairy products, but are kept indoors in very small spaces.

Faith schools: schools run by a particular religion rather than by the state.

Famine: starvation owing to drastic, far-reaching food shortage.

Fertility: being able to conceive a child.

Foetus: fertilised ovum at about eleven weeks when the organs have developed.

Fossil fuels: a hydrocarbon used as a fuel, like natural gas, petroleum, and coal.

Fostering: the taking of a child from a different family into a family home and bringing them up with the rest of the new family.

Freedom of choice: being able to choose to do whatever you want.

Free-range farming: farming that allows the animals to roam free and behave naturally.

Fur trade: the business of farming or hunting wild animals for their fur to be made into clothing.

G

Gender: another word for a person's sex.

Generation gap: a difference between the views of young people and their parents.

Genetic modification: plants and animals that have had their natural make up altered by scientists.

Geneva Conventions: rules about war and the treatment of prisoners and civilians.

Gift: the idea that a child is God's gift to humans.

Global warming: the scientific concept that the world is getting warmer.

Greenhouse effect: the trapping of heat from the sun in the lower atmosphere due to an increase in carbon dioxide, methane and other pollutantion.

Groups: people joining together.

H

Handicap: a physical or mental disability.

Harmony: living in peace with others.

Holy war: fighting for a religious cause or God probably controlled by a religious leader.

Human Fertilisation and Embryology Act (1990): the amendment to the Abortion Act (1967) that reduced time limit to 24 weeks.

Hunting: the chasing of animals to kill them, which may be done for food, protection or human pleasure.

I

Individuals: persons acting on their own.

Influence of parents: how values and opinions are passed on to children.

Influence of the media: newspapers, television, films can reinforce or break down stereotypes.

Initiation: being entered formally into a religion.

International action: action taken by a group of countries to help conserve the environment.

Ivory trade: the sale of ivory from elephants' tusks, often illegally.

J

Jihad: Arabic word meaning 'to struggle'. The greater jihad is an individual's struggle for spiritual perfection. The lesser jihad is a just war in defence of Islam.

Just War: a war that the Christian Church defines as acceptable: must fit certain criteria.

Justice: bringing about what is right, fair, according to the law or making up for what has been done wrong.

L

Law: rules in a country that govern how people live.

Lifestyle: the way people live that reflects their values and attitudes.

M

Marginalisation: the social process of becoming or being isolated and left out.

Media: the organisations which convey information to the public, especially television and the printed press.

Miracle of life: the idea that life is wonderful, amazing or special.

Moral codes: moral rules by which a person decides to live.

N

NATO: North Atlantic Treaty Organisation, an alliance formed to prevent war in Europe.

Natural disasters: disasters caused by nature, e.g. earthquakes, volcanoes.

Natural habitats: the places where species of plants or animals live in the wild.

Natural resources: the various things that the Earth provides for human usage, such as oil, gas, etc.

Non-biodegradable: not able to be broken down by the environment.

Nuclear proliferation: nuclear weapons spreading to other countries and getting more numerous.

Nuclear weapons: weapons that work by a nuclear reaction that devastate huge areas and kill large numbers of people.

O

Ohito Declaration: a statement of religious concern for the protection of the environment.

Oil spills: leaking of oil into the environment, usually the sea.

Origins of life: how life began.

Ozone layer: a layer of ozone in the upper atmosphere that absorbs most of the sun's ultraviolet radiation. Being destroyed by CFCs.

P

Pacifism: the belief of people who refuse to take part in war and any other form of violence.

Peace: an absence of conflict which leads to happiness and harmony.

Peace keeping force: troops sent by a group of countries to act as a buffer between warring parties, or to keep the peace after hostilities cease.

Peer pressure: influence exerted by friends on each other.

Pesticides: substances (poison) used to destroy insects and pests that attack crops.

Pollution: the contamination of something, especially the environment.

Positive discrimination: treating people more favourably because they have been discriminated against in the past.

Poverty: being poor; not having sufficient resources to live.

Prejudice: thinking badly of someone because of the group he/she belongs to.

Preservation: look after the environment and life in order to keep it safe.

Pressure groups: collections of people outside government who campaign for changes in society.

Pro-choice: in favour of a woman's right to choose an abortion.

Pro-life: opposed to abortion; in favour of the life of the foetus.

Proliferation: spreading to other countries and getting more numerous.

Purpose: the goal of life and the reason for living.

Q

Quakers: members of the Society of Friends, a Christian denomination.

Quality of life: a measure of fulfilment.

R

Race: usually used to refer to people of the same skin colour, ethnic group or nationality.

Racism: showing prejudice against someone because of their ethnic group or nationality.

Recycling: reusing old products to make new ones.

Red Crescent: the same as the Red Cross. National Red Crescent Societies are found predominantly in Muslim countries.

Red Cross: a humanitarian agency that helps people suffering from war or other disasters.

Refugees: people who flee from their homes seeking safety elsewhere.

Relationships: a relationship is an association among two or more people.

Religion: a set of beliefs, values and practices based on the teaching of a spiritual leader.

Religious prejudice: prejudice based on religion or beliefs.

Responsibility: duty; the idea that we are in charge of our own actions.

Rights: the legal or moral entitlements to do or not to do something.

S

Sacred: holy, previous because given by God.

Sanctity of life: life is sacred because it is God-given.

Scapegoating: blaming certain groups for problems in society.

Secular: not religious.

Severe weather: extreme weather events such as hurricanes, tornadoes, etc.

Sexism: prejudice and discrimination based on a person's gender (usually a woman).

Society: a grouping of people in a country.

Spirituality: a sense of something that is outside normal human experience.

Spring Harvest: annual inter-denominational Christian conference with the main events being held at the Butlins resorts at Skegness and Minehead.

Stereotyping: having an over-simplified mental image of people and applying it to everyone in a group.

Stewardship: the idea that believers have a duty to look after the environment on behalf of God.

Suffering: pain or distress.

Sustainable development: development that takes into consideration the impact on the natural world for future generations.

T

Taizé: a place in France where monks welcome the visit of young people.

Terrorism: the unlawful use of violence, usually against innocent civilians, to achieve a political goal.

Throwaway society: a term referring to the wastefulness.

Tolerance: respecting the beliefs and practices of others.

Toxic chemicals: poisonous chemicals.

U

United Nations (UN): an organisation set up at the end of World War II to prevent war by discussing problems between countries.

Unwanted children: unplanned pregnancies.

Upbringing: a person's rearing and education during childhood.

V

Value of the individual: the importance of every human being.

Vegan: a person who will not use any animal product.

Vegetarianism: the belief held by people who do not eat meat.

Viable: the point at which a foetus could survive if it were to be born.

Victims of war: people who are harmed or suffer as a result of war.

Vivisection: the cutting up of animals for scientific experiments.

W

'War on Terror': action taken after 9/11 to tighten security, prevent future attacks and destroy terrorist organisations.

Weapons of mass destruction (WMD): weapons that can kill large numbers of people and/or cause great damage.

Wonder: marvelling at the complexity and beauty of the universe.

Worship: ceremony or prayers showing love and devotion to a deity, an idol or sacred object.

Z

Zoos: places in which wild animals are kept to display to the public.

Index